# Database Design and Implementat

To the silent majority of non-giant computer users...

# Database Design and Implementation

## on maxi- and mini-computers

Daniel Martin

VAN NOSTRAND REINHOLD COMPANY

New York — Cincinnati — Toronto — London — Melbourne

© Van Nostrand Reinhold Co. Ltd., 1980

First published in 1977 by Bordas, Paris
as *Bases de Données: methodes pratiques*

**Published by Van Nostrand Reinhold Company Ltd.,
Molly Millars Lane, Wokingham, Berkshire, England**

*Published in 1980 by Van Nostrand Reinhold Company,
A Division of Litton Educational Publishing Inc.,
135 West 50th Street, New York, NY 10020, USA*

*Van Nostrand Reinhold Limited,
1410 Birchmount Road, Scarborough, Ontario, M1P 2E7,
Canada*

*Van Nostrand Reinhold Australia Pty. Limited,
17 Queen Street, Mitcham, Victoria 3132, Australia*

**Library of Congress Cataloging in Publication Data**


Martin, Daniel, ingenieur IDN
    Database design and implementation.
    Translation of Bases de donnees.
    1. Data base management.  I.  Title.
QA76.9.D3M3513        001.64'25        80 – 12122
ISBN 0 – 442 – 30429 – 3
ISBN 0 – 442 – 30430 – 7 (pbk.)

# Preface

So far, very few in-depth write-ups about database methodology have been published. The data processing press features articles about one detail or another of this vast subject. Some authors seem to take pleasure in describing the difficulty — or the mathematical aspects — of database development and implementation: it seems that very high costs just have to be incurred in the areas of software development manpower, computer processing power, memory and disk storage sizes; in addition, it sometimes seems that only professional mathematicians can understand database management.

For many computer users databases remain myths; in fact, 90% of the computers used for business data processing belong to the 'mini' and 'small' or 'medium-size' category. Somehow, this seems to discourage their users from seriously considering database implementation. This book addresses just those users, the silent majority of non-giant computer users. It contains actual design, programming and implementation methods specifically oriented towards databases.

These methods have, for the most part, been developed and tried by the author: they are working techniques, not theory. In addition, this book does not attempt to be an encyclopedia or a treatise on databases: the author does not believe that the state of the art is advanced enough for such an undertaking. Rather, this is a collection of ideas for efficient database design and implementation on most existing computers and minicomputers by systems analysts—not *all* ideas, but a few practical ones.

Furthermore, in order to achieve simplicity and ease of understanding, the presentation uses easy-to-generalize examples rather than difficult-to-apply theories.

In most installations, data processing (abbreviated to DP) today remains an automatic processing of repeated, simple operations such as: copy this piece of data from file A to file B, add AMOUNT to TOTAL, print this statement, etc. Business DP is mainly used for such applications as payroll, invoicing, inventory accounting: it is a mechanization of high-volume, relatively easy-to-perform tasks, particularly as it addresses companies at the lowest clerical levels. Until now DP has turned its back on the needs of managers to the extent that all the hardware, software and operational procedures have been specifically designed to process a high volume of *details*; consequently when it comes to synthetic summaries or answering unexpected questions, the sophisticated, costly DP organization feels ill at ease. We shall see that the database (abbreviated to DB) approach is both an answer to the managers' needs, while still suitable for high volume tasks. For example, this book contains simple yet general methods for answering such question as 'how many items number A2151 (yellow) did we sell in March to customers in OHIO who belong to category 85?'

As we shall see, no programming is involved, and the answer may be ready within minutes or seconds--a very easy operation!

This book is concerned with business databases, excluding such subjects as document retrieval ('find all write-ups about the following subject. . .'), for example.

Two different types of database are described. First, *closed* databases, which are simple to understand and implement, and quite similar to 'disk files' (familiar to system analysts) are described. Second, the powerful, sophisticated *open* databases are presented, with instructions for designing one.

# Contents

# CHAPTER 1

# Definitions Related to Data

We hear a lot about databases, but few of those who speak about them can define precisely what a database is. Ill-defined concepts lead to inaccurate thinking, then to regrettable decisions. So, before we discuss databases, we will review two types of definition:

1. definitions of groups of data, regardless of how they are actually processed;
2. definitions of groups of data that have been brought together to be processed together.

## 1.1 DEFINITIONS OF DATA GROUPS

### 1.1.1 Databases

By definition, a database on a given subject is a collection of data on that subject that obeys three criteria:

exhaustivity (completeness),
non-redundancy,
appropriate structure.

Exhaustivity means that *all* the data about the subject are actually present in the database.

Non-redundancy means that each individual piece of data exists only *once* in the database.

Appropriate structure means that the data are stored in such a way as to minimize the cost of the expected processing and/or storage.

Note: The definition above is more general than the one some authors prefer; according to them, the only 'real' databases are those with an 'open' structure. Such databases allow for easy change of field dimensions (for example: increasing a given field's size from six to seven digits), for easy addition of *new* fields, for easy change in data linkage (for example: link a customer's record to all transactions performed on his account: invoices, payments, etc.) without recompiling existing programs. In fact, the ease of evolution associated with open databases is very costly in terms of processing time, memory space and disk storage; we will discover that closed (that is 'non-open') databases are often an acceptable solution.

In short, we will consider both closed and open DB's as 'real'. The following example will clarify the definition.

*Example 1.1* 'Customer database used for invoicing and the follow-up of resulting payments':

Exhaustivity implies the presence, within the database, of *all* the information pertaining to a given customer, whether it belongs to an invoice (name, address, etc.) or to a payment (date of payment, amount, etc.). It also implies the presence of this information for all customers who may have outstanding invoices.

Non-redundancy excludes the possibility that certain pieces of data exist more than once within the database. For example, if the 'payments-due' file of the database contains the name and address of each debtor, and if this information is already stored in the 'customer' file, it is therefore redundant.

This example shows that redundancy should be minimized, and avoided completely if possible. However, in many cases, absolute non-redundancy is difficult to achieve, or may cause poor processing speed. To demonstrate this difficulty, let us consider in the above example the case of the 'customer number', used as identification key, for the records of both the customer file and the payments-due file. We will demonstrate, using file structure examples, what may result from strict non-redundancy. And we will take advantage of this first discussion of file structures to present a technique of major importance in the field of databases: the use of *pointers*.

Let us define a pointer. Assume that the database uses two files, the 'customer' file and the 'payments-due' file. Each customer file record contains a

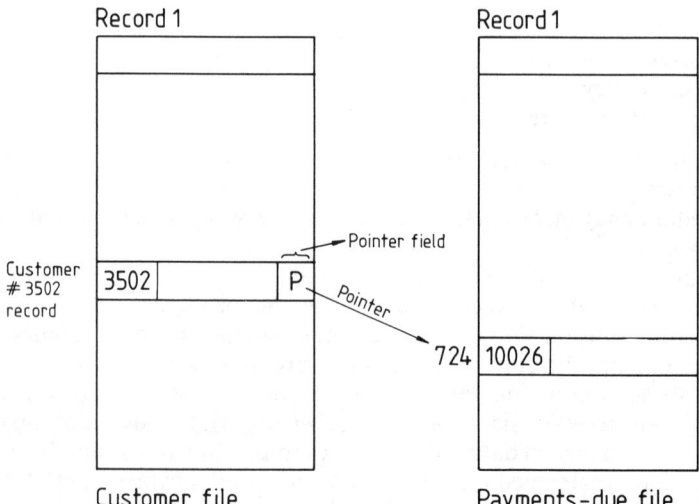

Fig. 1.1    Record layouts.

customer number, customer data such as the associated name and address, and an extra numeric field called P. Each payment-due record describes the invoice that caused the payment: invoice number, date, amount, etc. To link customer number 3502 with the payment expected for invoice 10026 that was sent to him, and which is the 724th record of the payments-due file, we store the number 724 (the 'address' of the record) in the P field of the customer file record of customer 3502 (see Fig. 1.1). This figure uses an arrow to represent the pointer, stored in field P. Thus, we will say that a customer record *points* to a payment-due record, and that field P is the *pointer* field. P contains, a record number, relative to the payments-due file. This must be a random access-type file.

Now that we know what a pointer is, let us proceed with our demonstration of the consequences of redundancy/non-redundancy, using the following examples.

*Example 1.2: Non-redundant Structure.* Several invoices may have been sent to an individual customer. So, if we want to avoid redundancy, we may store within the customer record a pointer for each invoice/payment-due to be found in the payments-due file (Fig. 1.2).

*Example 1.3: Non-redundant Structure.* The structure above has an obvious disadvantage: if the number of invoices per customer is not limited, it may only be implemented using variable-size records, as the number of pointer fields may be considerable. However many computer operating systems will not accomodate variable-size disk records, especially in random-access files—and a customer file has to be a random-access file.

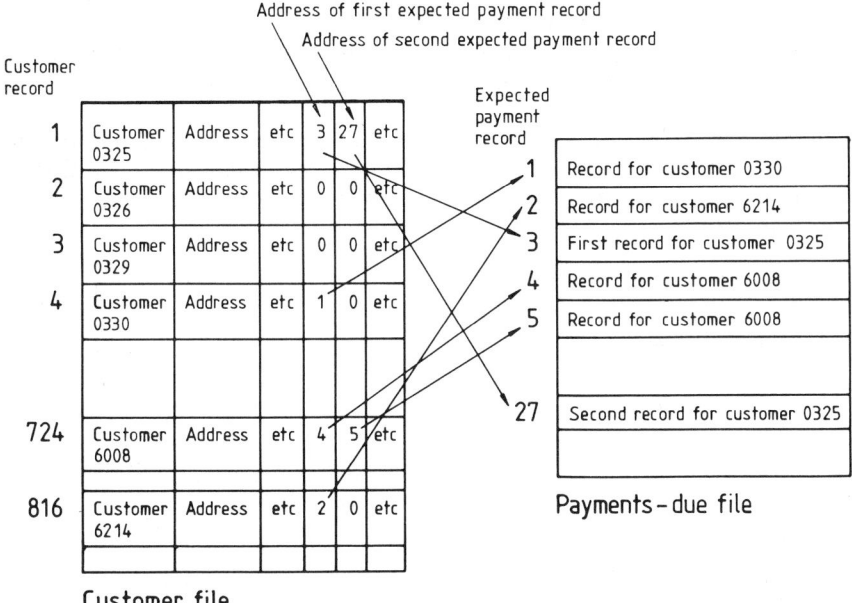

Fig. 1.2    Note: a 0 pointer indicates that no payment is expected.

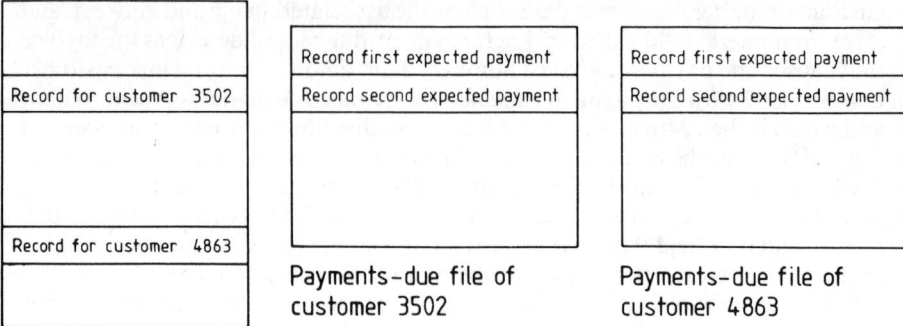

Record for customer 3502

Record for customer 4863

Customer file

Record first expected payment

Record second expected payment

Payments-due file of
customer 3502

Record first expected payment

Record second expected payment

Payments-due file of
customer 4863

Fig. 1.3

So, a second structure may be considered: suppress the pointer field(s) and use a small disk file associated with each customer. Assuming this file can expand as required, that each of its records contains one expected payment, and that its name can be computed knowing the customer number with which it is associated, then this is a theoretically viable structure (Fig. 1.3). Unfortunately, this structure has many defects:

if 50 000 customers have expected payments, we may have to store 50 000 small disk files: most storage devices and/or operating systems will not tolerate that;

disk space waste may be considerable, as the small disk files may not be full of expected payment records;

obtaining a list of all expected payments may take a lot of processing time, as the cost of opening/closing a disk file may be that of several disk accesses.

*Example 1.4: Non-redundant Structure.* Assume we go back to the structure of Fig. 1.1 and add a second pointer (P2) to the payments-due record; P2, if greater than zero, will point towards the *next* invoice/payments-due record of the same customer. This is a satisfactory structure (Fig. 1.4).

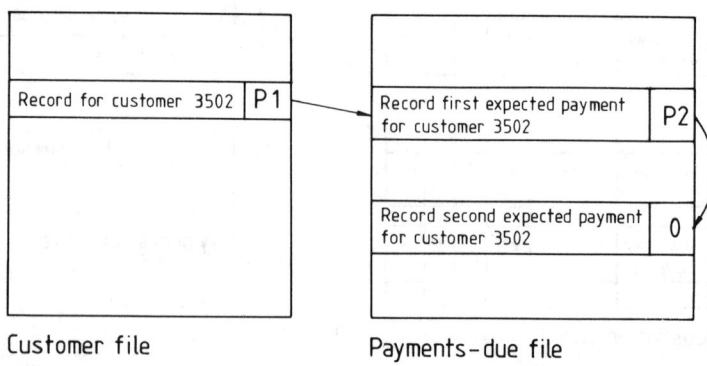

Customer file              Payments-due file

Fig. 1.4

4

The structure of the payments-due file is often referred to as a LIST structure, as the records linked by the pointers P2 may be listed in the order in which they where added.

However, if one of the purposes of the database is to produce a report of expected payments that includes customer information, we have to scan the entire customer file. For each customer whose P pointer is greater than zero we will find one or several expected payments in the other file. The problem is that, if only 10% of customers have at least one payments-due record, we will read nine useless customer records for each useful one. Another serious problem is of database integrity; what if, (due to erroneous operator manipulation or faulty software) the P pointers are lost or become corrupted? We remain with a file full of payments-due records, without knowing for certainty to which customer a given record belongs!

*Example 1.5: Redundant Structure.* We can avoid the drawbacks of the previous structure by adding the customer number as a supplementary field to each record of the payments-due file (Fig. 1.5). The storage is now partially redundant. And since we accept some redundancy, we will also accelerate the process of retrieving debtor customers; a table of debtors will be created in the 'header' portion of the file, to associate the number of each debtor customer with the address of his first payments-due record. This in turn will contain a pointer to the next payment-due record of the same customer, etc.

The records of the payments-due file do not *physically* point toward the associated customer file records, as no such pointer exists. However, as they include the necessary customer number each required customer file record can be retrieved using ordinary software search techniques. We can describe this

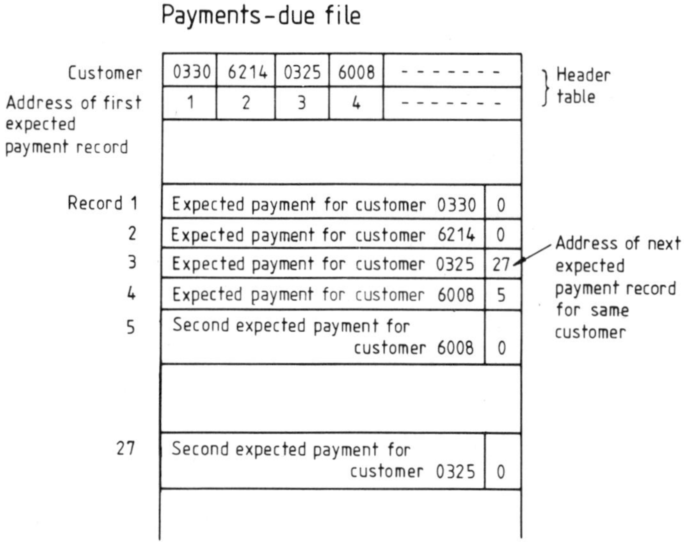

Payments-due file

Fig. 1.5

pointerless pointing technique as 'implicit pointing', and it is based on the existence of record search keys instead of record address pointers.

The above examples demonstrate the need for correct file structures.

*Structure 1* is a convenient means to find out what payments-due records exist for a given customer, and where they are located. But unless we use variable-size customer records, it offers a *limited* amount of debit records. In addition, it wastes some of the space provided for the address of debit records.

*Structure 2* wastes even more space.

*Structure 3* is unsafe: there is a danger of losing pointers.

*Structure 4* saves disk space but is redundant and requires more complicated software to find and update the payments-due records. It is, nevertheless, the best of the four structures in terms of data storage efficiency and safety.


### 1.1.2 Comparison of the Database and the Classical Approaches

A company which has used data processing for a long time has employed:

    a card-oriented computer;
    a magnetic tape-oriented computer;
    a disk-oriented computer.

A card or magnetic tape-oriented computer offered a limited core storage volume. On-line storage using a fast drum or disk was very expensive and reserved for work files (for sorting, for example) or for small permanent tables. Nowadays, the cost of both memory and disk storage is decreasing rapidly; many data processing users can afford to have tens or hundreds of millions of characters on-line.

Because of this evolution, most applications were designed around *sequential* files, where the records were sorted in the order required for processing. A large percentage of processing time was used to sort card, tape, or even disk files. The computer would spend a lot of time reading and copying records that were not actually needed. In order to save time, the contents of the records were cut to the minimum required by the processing programs. Each application used its own record layouts; non-exhaustivity was the rule for record design. This resulted in redundancy; it was necessary to copy from file X of application A to file Y the data required by application B that used Y. As some of the data of X were also in Y redundancy was inevitable. File structures, however, were simple; so sequential storage prevailed; there were no pointers or header tables.

In short, data processing used non-exhaustive, redundant and unstructured files designed for specific applications. Computer interrogation was impossible, as:

    the data were dispersed among several files, some of which were not on-line;
    even if the data files were on-line, the absence of structure made searches very slow—and too expensive. Reading three files of 100 000 records each to answer a question was just not practical. In addition, a special

program had to be developed for that specific question, or that specific set of files.

Conclusions:

1. The relatively small number of databases used today is a result of historical conditions;
2. non-exhaustivity and the absence of structure are the two main differences between the database approach and the 'classical' approach;
3. computer interrogation, answering unprepared questions, and consolidating the synthetic results required by top managers need databases;
4. the on-line storage demanded by the database approach implies a large disk storage capacity; this is no longer expensive;
5. the database approach results in a different design of application files and programs.

In addition, we shall see below that database-oriented applications involve fewer programs and simpler execution procedures; this in turn provides better reliability. We shall also see that it is often possible to take into account *all the consequences* of an incoming transaction at one time, instead of updating several non-resident files in succession.

### 1.1.3 Logical File

We have seen that a database is the set of all the data about a given subject; we also want the entire database to be on-line for inquiries or updates. We know that, in order to structure the data, we have to build up *data groups* (we may, for example, link related data records with pointers).

A 'customer' database is exhaustive in two ways:

it contains all the data about a given customer;
it contains all the data for all the customers.

This second type of exhaustivity leads to the storage of many customer numbers, customer names and addresses, etc. The various customer data are stored together in a 'customer logical file', to contain for example, all the *stable* data items (number, name, address, etc.). A second logical file, the payments-due logical file will contain *unstable* data. The separation into two logical files results from the fundamental difference between the two data groups, from the standpoint of expected duration. It is, however, arbitrary, and the same application could be designed using other data partitions, based on different criteria.

Let us simply remember that a database can be subdivided into logical files; each file will contain *some* of the types of data for *all* existing records.

### 1.1.4 Logical Record

The previous subdivision of the database was: '*all* customers/*some* types of data'. If we now divide the database into parts such as: '*one* customer/*all* types of data for that customer' we have defined a partition into *logical records*. Each logical record will contain a customer number, name, address and all the associated payments-due data, so the database will contain one logical record for each customer.

### 1.1.5 Physical Files and Records

Logical files are *abstract* groups of data. Actual data are stored using *physical* files. A physical file is a set of data stored on a physical medium such as a disk. It contains a number of data subsets (called *physical records*) which have an identical layout. So, if the physical record for one customer includes the number, name and address, the physical customer file will include all the physical customer records.

The method of establishing the contents of database files takes into account the exhaustivity and non-redundancy of the data. First, we must define the contents of the logical files; these in turn can be used to define physical files. To achieve storage and processing efficiency, one logical file will frequently result in several physical files with complementary contents. Sometimes, the same physical file will store data originating from different logical files. In general, disk files have fixed-length records; so if various types of logical records are stored in the same physical file, they must have the same length. Conceivably, some logical records can be stored using several fixed-length physical records.

*Example 1.6* Storing the records of the header table in the payments-due file will avoid opening two files (a table file, or a payments-due file). This may be an advantage, as it saves memory space and sometimes also processing time (each OPEN or CLOSE operation results in the execution of hundreds of instructions, and one or more disk accesses). In addition, the number of files that can be opened at the same time by a given program is limited on some computers or minicomputers.

### 1.1.6 Field

A data field is a physical group of characters that represent an individual item of data called a *logical field*. A physical field is a set of consecutive words, characters or bits depending on the computer and the programming language. A physical record contains a whole number of physical fields.

During its definition phase, the contents of a database are first described as a set of functional results; then these are defined in terms of logical fields, and the latter subsequently grouped into logical records.

## 1.2 DEFINITIONS RELATED TO PROCESSING

The following definitions are stated briefly to introduce the terminology that will be used to discuss file structures.

8

### 1.2.1 Disk Page

Disk file space is generally reserved in multiples of a minimum quantity called a *page*. The page size varies depending on such factors as storage technology, systems software and user specifications.

The word 'page' is used to avoid such hardware-oriented words as 'track', 'cylinder', etc. The pages of a given physical file may be contiguous or non-contiguous.

### 1.2.2 Block and Buffer

Data are transferred between memory and disks in multiples of a minimal quantity called *block* or *segment*. In general, the page size is a multiple of the block size; this in turn is a multiple of the physical record size. However, the system software will sometimes add a few header or trailer characters to each page, block or record in order to describe it or to link it to other pages, blocks or records.

The memory area used to store the block(s) that come from (or go to) the disk is known as a *buffer* area. When a program performs a READ statement, a block of data is taken from the disk and copied into the buffer. Then, if there are several physical records in each block, a splitting operation selects one physical record from the buffer and copies it into the record definition area of the program. So, reading several consecutive records will result in fewer disk accesses.

When a buffer is unique for a given file, it is both an 'input' and 'output' buffer. Sometimes two buffers are available: one for input, and one for output; occasionally there is a *single* such buffer pair for *all* the files open at any one time in the computer.

Most database management systems (DBMS's) employ a memory area called a *buffer pool* to store the individual file buffers in simultaneous use. The buffer pool management algorithm is one of the keys of the database management system's efficiency. In this respect, the computer's overall virtual memory page-swapping strategy:

> should be considered carefully before decisions are made regarding the buffer pool management algorithm;
> should be tuned together with the buffer pool size after the initial database management system implementation.

# CHAPTER 2

# Data Representation and Storage Methods

Note: This chapter is the only one where some knowledge of mathematics is required. Hopefully, the reader will find it elementary.

We have seen, in the previous chapter, that the database approach requires the presence of all data on-line, both to retrieve and to update. As a result, the amount of disk storage required may be considerable, the volume of data transferred between the processor and the disks may be high, and the processor time required to search through the database may be costly.

The purpose of this chapter is to describe a few cost-saving methods, oriented towards volume minimization. First we briefly describe the straightforward techniques known as *full length* and *code* representations, then proceed with a detailed description of techniques particularly suited to databases.

## 2.1  FULL-LENGTH STORAGE

This is the simplest possible data representation and storage method; a word or text (series of words), or one or several numbers are simply written using the letters, digits and signs required. Although this is a very simple operation it unfortunately leads to cumbersome storage and lends itself badly to retrieval operations; the comparison of character strings is not very easy to program (except with specific languages and correctly justified strings); and the spacing and spelling of words, and the use of abbreviations, may result in data-search unpredictability.

All keypunch operators know that copying or verifying alphanumeric data is slower and less reliable than copying numeric codes.

## 2.2  REPRESENTING DATA WITH CODES

This method consists of representing a concept with a numeric code. We use customer numbers, item numbers, record type codes, etc. Codes have the disadvantage of all symbols in that they are not self-explanatory. But they also have many advantages:

they are not cumbersome: a two-digit code can represent a 40-character legend string;

they are easy to compare during retrieval operations;

they are easy to enter and verify.

*All the techniques discussed below are in fact coding techniques.*

## 2.3 VOCABULARY AND ALPHABET

Consider the following example: the 'item' file of a manufacturer of gear boxes. A preliminary evaluation of the volume of the file produced the following results:

number of items: 10 000,

item record size:

numeric data (part number, price, size, etc.): 30 characters,

alphabetic data (part name): 30 characters,

total file size: 10 000 × (30 + 30) = 600 000 characters

A survey of actual part names led to the conclusion that some names or qualifiers appeared more frequently than others: wheel, pinion, sprocket, gear, case, bearing, shaft, etc. A list of these names was made; there were only 25, and they represented all the important words used in the part names. It was then decided to code each important word using one letter: wheel = A; pinion = B; sprocket = C; etc.

The part-name field was reduced from 30 to five characters, which represented five (maximum) important words. The file size was thus reduced by 10 000 (30 − 5) = 250 000 characters, a little over 40%, which could now reside on a single disk cylinder, thus reducing the number of arm movements and accelerating the accesses. A conversion subprogram was developed and included in the part-name printing programs.

This example introduces the following concepts: 10 000 part names can be built up using only 25 words; the *vocabulary* is said to comprise 25 words. Storage economy can be achieved associating one code to each word.

The previous example contained 25 such letter codes, which shows, surprisingly, how small the vocabularies used in many files are. Very often, they make up a set of 100 words or less. It is then very convenient to code the various words using a two or three-digit code, which can be used as an actual *address* in the conversion table. For example, if

| | | |
|---|---|---|
| 16 = Low-noise | (16th table entry) |
| 08 = Gearbox | ( 8th table entry) |
| 21 = Light alloy | (21st table entry) |
| 05 = Case | ( 5th table entry) |

then 1608210500 = low-noise gearbox light alloy case.

It is often found that conversions are not required for all the processing operations; the internal, non-visible, computer data handling may be performed using codes. Only the external representations (data entry, printout) need be converted.

We can retain the following definitions:

the *vocabulary* is the set of all the words required to build up the descriptions of the concepts to be handled;

the *alphabet* is the set of codes used to represent the vocabulary, with the rule that one word is associated with one code and vice versa.

Note:

1.  the 'words' can be actual words, sequences of symbols or short sentences; the only constraint is that they may not be split.
2.  The codes of an alphabet can be letters, groups of digits, etc.
3.  Associating one word with one code is an important source of savings in disk storage space, disk channel transfer time, processor time (compare and move instructions, sorting operations).
4.  The notions of vocabulary and alphabet imply the non-redundancy and exhaustivity of the set of words used to build up the concepts.
5.  The above definitions (vocabulary, alphabet) apply to the realm of data-bases; different definitions are used in another data processing-related domain: the theory of languages.

## 2.4 BASE

The data representation method explained above is suitable for vocabularies limited to a few hundred words. But it can be generalized and extended to vocabularies that are arbitrarily large and still remain practical to use.

*Example 2.1* The prices of the items of a file are expressed in dollars and cents; the number of cents is always a multiple of 25 cents. Prices range from 50 cents to 80 dollars.

*First storage technique:* use four digits to store the price field.

*Second storage technique:* let us associate with each price $P$ an integer $x$ such that:

$$x = \frac{P - 0.50}{0.25} \quad \text{or} \quad P = 0.25\,x + 0.50 \quad (T)$$

which means that

$$x = 0 \text{ if } P = 0.50$$
$$x = 1 \text{ if } P = 0.75$$
$$x = 2 \text{ if } P = 1.00$$

$$x = 318 \text{ if } P = 80.00$$

This storage technique uses a three-digit field to store the price $P$ if we store $x$ instead of $P$. It saves 25% of the space. In this example, the vocabulary comprises 319 words, so the alphabet has 319 codes. We can use a special numbering system to represent this set of codes; a numbering system in base 319. In this system, each number $x$ is represented by a single digit. We shall not (of course) invent new and strange signs to represent the digits beyond nine. We can use the natural representation of numbers available in our computer, three-digit values of $x$, and convert $x$'s to $P$'s or $P$'s to $x$'s using formulas ($T$). We shall note that the *base B* of a vocabulary is the number of its words. In this base, each word is coded with a one-digit number ranging from 0 to $B-1$. To calculate $B$ and establish the ($T$) formulas:

1. Obtain the minimum ($m$) and maximum ($M$) values of the number $N$ to be represented.
2. Obtain the 'step' '$S$' of $N$: $N$ is an arithmetic progression.
3. Calculate $B = \dfrac{M - m}{S} + 1$
4. The formulas ($T1$) are:

   coding/packing: $\qquad x = \dfrac{N - m}{S}$

   $\hfill (T)$

   decoding/unpacking $\quad N = S \times x + m$

## 2.5 DATA PACKING: MULTIPLE BASES

Generally speaking, the use of compact codes to represent data is called *data packing*. It is particularly useful in the area of data transmission. A data transmission line has a maximum throughput. The ratio

$$\frac{\text{Number of useful characters transmitted}}{\text{Total number of characters transmitted}}$$

measures how efficiently the line is used. Thus, the transmission of many 'space' characters in succession should be replaced by the transmission of TAB characters, or of a special character followed by a two-digit number representing the number of spaces. There are special hardware devices that automatically pack identical consecutive characters. These devices are inserted between the MODEM and the user's computer or terminal (Fig. 2.1). But the interest of data packing is not limited to data transmission; we have seen in the previous paragraph that it can also reduce storage costs and the load on disk channels.

The method discussed above was suitable for a single field. *It can now be extended to an entire record.* A record is an ordered set of fields. Each field is associated with a specific vocabulary, which in turn is associated with all the different concepts that can be represented in that field.

To a given field we know how to associate a base B, the number of different vocabulary words. The first word will be coded 'zero', the second 'one', the last:

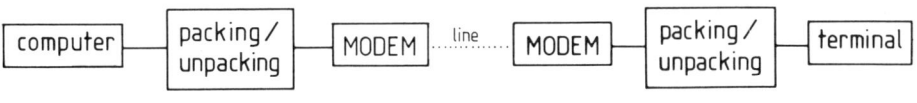

Fig. 2.1

'B-1'. That seems easy for numeric fields, but not for alphanumeric fields, as the number of words of such a field is not always known. Fortunately, in most cases, the following statement is true: a *large* percentage of the words encountered build up a *small* vocabulary. We know that a *small* vocabulary can be coded (see section 2.3). We can then add a 'special' code-character to our alphabet and use it as a begin-and-end delimiter around the strings of characters that represent the 'rare' words; those rare words can then be stored with their natural, full-length string representation, a technique that will prove useful in some large databases. It is the last step of the vocabulary definition process:

> build a file of all the words;
> count the number of occurrences of each word;
> decide what words to code, the rest being represented in full length.

Throughout the rest of this chapter we shall assume that the coding process has been performed for each field of the record in question.

Let us consider a record with $p$ fields. Each field ($i$) has been converted using formulas ($T$) and contains an integer $n_i$ ranging from 0 to $B_i - 1$ (where $B_i$ is the base of field ($i$)). We can pack the record field integers $n_1, n_2, \ldots n_p$ into a single integer $N$.

Unpacking will subsequently convert $N$ into $n_1, n_2, \ldots n_p$.


### 2.5.1 Packing

Packing will be achieved using the 'multiple base formula':

$$N = n_1 + B_1 \star n_2 + B_1 \star B_2 \star n_3 + \ldots$$
$$\ldots + B_1 \star B_2 \star \ldots \star B_l \star n_{l+1} + \ldots$$
$$\ldots + B_1 \star B_2 \star \ldots \star B_{p-1} \star n_p$$

where $\star$ is the multiplication sign.


### 2.5.2 Interpretation of the Packing Formula

*Example 2.2*  Assume that the record contains three fields of ten concepts (words) each. The concepts will be called 'unit', 'ten' and 'hundred'. We have:

$$p = 3$$
$$B_1 = B_2 = B_3 = 10$$

To pack $n_1 = 2$ units, $n_2 = 4$ tens, $n_3 = 6$ hundreds we will calculate

$$N = 2 + 10 \star 4 + 10 \star 10 \star 6 = 642.$$

$N$ is a three-digit integer:
   the first digit, in base $B_1 = 10$ is $n_1 = 2$ (rightmost digit);
   the second digit, in base $B_2 = 10$ is $n_2 = 4$, shifted one position to the left of $n_1$;
   the third digit, in base $B_3 = 10$, is $n_3 = 6$, shifted one position (in base $B_1$) to

the left of $n_1$, then one position (in base $B_2$) to the left of $n_2$.

Comments:

1.  Using the multiple base formula amounts to creating a $p$ – digit integer $N$. The rightmost (low-order) digit is written in base $B_1$, the next digit is written in base $B_2$, etc. The representation of $N$ using this multiple-base approach builds up a number, $N$, with digits written in different bases. The *arithmetical value* of $N$ represents the values of all the fields of the original record; it exists independently of the multiple-base *representation*; it ranges from 0 to $B_1 \star B_2 \star \ldots \star B_p - 1$ (in the previous example, $N$ ranged from 0 to 999).
2.  The length of a physical record is the sum of the lengths of its fields, it is independent of their order. Similarly, no matter how the record representation, $N$, is stored in the computer, the space it requires *is the same*; it is the space required to store $N_{max} = B_1 \star B_2 \star \ldots \star B_{p-1}$. (The product $B_1 \star \ldots \star B_p$ is commutative).
3.  The value, $N$, requires a 'record storage base' $B = B_1 \star B_2 \star \ldots \star B_p$. This means that the number of different possible records is $B$, which is the product of the numbers of different individual field values. Therefore the compactness of this packing technique is *the* maximum. No matter how the actual computer works (with bits, bytes, or words) it is impossible to achieve more compact packing.

### 2.5.3 Unpacking

Unpacking is performed using a technique called 'successive remainders':

*Step 1:* $n_1$ is the remainder when $N$ is divided by $B_1$ (for example: in the usual decimal representation, the rightmost digit of a number is the remainder of the division of the number by 10). Let $Q_1$ be the quotient of the division:

$$N = Q_1 \star B_1 + n_1.$$

*Step 2:* Divide $Q_1$ by $B_2$: the quotient is $Q_2$ and the remainder $n_2$.

*Step 3:* Divide $Q_2$ by $B_3$: the quotient is $Q_3$ and the remainder $n_3$, etc.

*Example 2.3*   We have a five-field record (Table 2.1). The actual respective field values are:

$$x_1 = 4 \quad x_2 = 8.3 \quad x_3 = 16 \quad x_4 = 0 \quad x_5 = 1500$$

### 2.5.4 Further Packing

Let us first calculate the bases, using the formula of section 2.4:

$$B = \frac{M - m}{S} + 1$$

(See Table 2.2).

**Table 2.1**

| Field number | Minimum value | Maximum value | Step | Comment |
|---|---|---|---|---|
| 1 | $-2$ | 16 | 2 | number $-2, 0, 2, 4, \ldots, 16$ |
| 2 | 0 | 20.4 | 0.1 | number $0, 0.1, 0.2, \ldots, 20.4$ |
| 3 | 0 | 39 | 1 ⎫ | Characters of a 'reduced' |
| 4 | 0 | 39 | 1 ⎬ | alphabet |
| 5 | 1000 | 1999 | 1 ⎭ | number $1000, 1001, \ldots, 1999$ |

**Table 2.2**

| Field number | Calculation | Base |
|---|---|---|
| 1 | $\dfrac{16 - (-2)}{2} + 1$ | 10 |
| 2 | $\dfrac{20.4 - 0}{0.1} + 1$ | 205 |
| 3 and 4 | $\dfrac{39 - 0}{1} + 1$ | 40 |
| 5 | $\dfrac{1999 - 1000}{1} + 1$ | 1000 |

Now calculate the $n_i$ digits using the $(T)$ formula of section 2.4:

$$n_i = \frac{x_i - m_i}{S}$$

$$n_1 = \frac{4 - (-2)}{2} = 3$$

$$n_2 = \frac{8.3 - 0}{0.1} = 83$$

$$n_3 = \frac{16 - 0}{1} = 16$$

$$n_4 = \frac{0 - 0}{1} = 0$$

$$n_5 = \frac{1500 - 1000}{1} = 500$$

We can compute $N$, using the multiple base formula:

$$N = 3 + 10 \star 83 + (10 \star 205) \star 16 + (10 \star 205 \star 40) \star$$
$$\star\ 0 + (10 \star 205 \star 40 \star 40) \star 500$$
$$N = 3 + 830 + 32800 + 0 + 1640000000$$
$$N = 1640033633$$

### 2.5.5 Further Unpacking

Divide 1640033633 by 10:

    $Q_1 = 164003363$          and $n_1 = 3$

Divide $Q_1$ by 205:

    $Q_2 = 800016$          and $n_2 = 83$

Divide $Q_2$ by 40:

    $Q_3 = 20000$          and $n_3 = 16$

Divide $Q_3$ by 40:

    $Q_4 = 500$          and $n_4 = 0$

Divide $Q_4$ by 1000:

    $Q_5 = 0$          and $n_5 = 500$

It is now easy to find the initial $x_i$ values; apply formula $(T)$ : $x_i = n_i \star S + m_i$.

### 2.5.6 Storage Economy

Let us verify that the packing achieved in the above example leads to more compact storage than the natural representation of the computer. Assuming we have a byte-oriented computer where one byte = two digits or one digit + one sign (Table 2.3).

**Table 2.3**

| Field number | COBOL picture | Field size (bytes) |
|---|---|---|
| 1 | S99 | 1.5 |
| 2 | 99V9 | 1.5 |
| 3 and 4 | X | 1 (2 times) |
| 5 | 9999 | 2 |

Total unpacked record length: seven bytes

Now the maximum value of $N$ is

$B_1 \star B_2 \star B_3 \star B_4 \star B_5 - 1$, or

$10 \star 205 \star 40 \star 40 \star 1000 - 1 = 3280000000 - 1$

This ten-digit number requires five bytes: PICTURE 9(10).

## 2.6 PACKING USING MULTIPLE WORDS

The $N$ numbers are generally big; they may even have 50 digits. Some computers can handle such integers, others cannot. This section describes the technique to be used when a record to be packed results in an integer $N$ greater than the largest permitted integer, $M$. (The notion of an $M$ integer is often associated with that of a computer 'word': the name 'multiple word' packing comes from the need to use several words to store $N$.

For example, a computer such as the H 6000 has 36-bit words; When it stores an integer, one bit is used for the sign and 35 bits for the integer value. The base is then $2^{35}$. Therefore:

$$M = 2^{35} - 1 = 34359738367.$$

### 2.6.1 Technique

In the following discussion, we shall define a 'word' as the memory area that can store $M$, regardless of the computers' actual memory-access technique (word, byte, etc.).

Let $B_1, B_2, \ldots B_p$ be the $p$ bases associated with the fields of the record to be packed. Let us multiply $B_1 \star B_2 \star B_3 \star \ldots$ until this product is the largest such product that still 'fits' within $M + 1$ : let $B_h$ be the last base of this product. By definition:

$$B_1 \star B_2 \star \ldots \star B_h \leqslant M + 1$$

1. If $h = p$, the entire record 'fits' within one word; multiple word packing is not required.
2. If $h < p$, let

$$R = \frac{M + 1}{B_1 \star B_2 \star \ldots \star B_h}$$

   where $R$ is an integer quotient.
3. If $R = 1$, the word must be considered 'full'; start packing into another word with base $B_{h+1}$, etc.
4. If $R > 1$, $R$ is the greatest additional base that can be packed in one word together with $B_1, B_2, \ldots B_h$.
5. If $R$ belongs to the remaining set of bases $\{B_{h+1} \ldots B_p\}$ ($R$ is a base $B_r$ of that set) exchange $B_r$ and $B_{h+1}$ : then $B_1, B_2, \ldots B_h, B_r$ can be packed together into one word:

$$\frac{M + 1}{B_1 \star \ldots \star B_h \star B_R} = 1$$

   this is case (3) above.
6. If there is a remaining base $B_x$ such that $B_x < R$, $B_x$ can be packed in the same word as $B_1, B_2, \ldots B_h$, a new $R$ can be calculated, etc.
7. If all remaining bases are greater than $R$, and since $R \geqslant 2$, any remaining base $B_x$ can be subdivided into two new bases $B_a$ and $R$ such that $B_a \star R \geqslant B_x$. In other words, we can store one part (with a base $R$) of the field asso-

ciated with $B_x$ in the first word and the other part (with a base $B_a$) in the second word. The field is then written using two digits, one in base $R$ and one in base $B_a$.

8. Continue packing bases into the second word, etc.

We can now describe the method to be used to write the number $n_x$ (in base $B_x$) as two digits in bases $R$ and $B_a$:

the first (low-order) digit, in base $R$ will be called $C_1$;
the other digit will be called $C_2$.

Since we must have

$$n_x = R \star C_2 + C_1$$

$C_2$ and $C_1$ are respectively the quotient and the remainder in the integer division of $n_x$ by $R$.

*Example 2.4*   Assume that our computer has words that can store integers in 31 bits: $M = 2^{31} - 1$. Further assume that, following the conversion of fields using formula $(T)$, the four fields of the record to be packed have bases such as:

| Field number | Base |
|---|---|
| 1 | $2^{20}$ |
| 2 | $2^{10}$ |
| 3 | $2^{5}$ |
| 4 | $2^{24}$ |

$B_1 < 2^{31}$, so $B_1$ fits in word 1; $B_1 \star B_2 = 2^{30} < 2^{31}$, so $B_1$ and $B_2$ fit in word 1; $B_1 \star B_2 \star B_3 = 2^{35} > 2^{31}$, so $B_3$ does not fit in word 1; Then

$$R = \frac{2^{31}}{2^{30}} = 2$$

and $B_3$ can be subdivided into

$$R = 2 \text{ and } B_a = B_3/R = 2^5/2 = 2^4.$$

A number of the third field can be written with two digits: the low-order digit, in base 2, will be stored in the first word together with fields 1 and 2; the high-order digit, in base $2^4 = 16$ will be in the second word, where $B_a \star B_4 = 2^4 \star 2^{24} < 2^{31}$, so $B_4$ fits into the word, and the record can therefore be packed into two words.

A number of field 3 will be subdivided into its two digits using a division by 2:

$$n_3 = 2 \star C_2 + C_1$$

For example, if we want to store

$$n_1 = 8 \qquad n_2 = 70 \qquad n_3 = 10 \qquad n_4 = 49$$

we calculate the values $N_1$ and $N_2$ of the two words like this:

$$N_1 = n_1 + B_1 \star n_2 + B_1 \star B_2 \star C_1$$
$$N_2 = C_2 + B_a \star n_4$$

that is:

$$10 = 2 \star C_2 + C_1 \rightarrow C_1 = 0, C_2 = 5$$
$$N_1 = 8 + 2^{20} \star 70 + 2^{20} \star 2^{10} \star 0$$
$$N_2 = 5 + 2^4 \star 49.$$

To unpack, we calculate $n_1$, $n_2$, $n_3$, $n_4$ from $N_1$ and $N_2$ in the following way:

Divide $N_1$ by $B_1$ giving $Q_1$ remainder $n_1$.
Divide $Q_1$ by $B_2$ giving $Q_2$ remainder $n_2$.
Divide $Q_2$ by $R$ giving 0 remainder $C_1$.
Divide $N_2$ by $B_a$ giving $n_4$ remainder $C_2$.
Compute $n_3 = C_1 + 2 \star C_2$

Note: In the above example, the same storage efficiency (that is, the record packed into two words) could be achieved by packing $B_1$ and $B_2$ (only) in word 1, then $B_3$ and $B_4$ in word 2. This would result in faster computations; we must therefore use the multiple word-packing technique intelligently!

## 2.7 WHEN IS DATA PACKING WORTHWHILE?

Data packing evidently saves disk and memory space. It also requires processor resources to pack and unpack. The following discussion is intended to help the analyst decide when and how he should use data packing.

### 2.7.1 The Cost of Packing

The cost elements of packing are:

1. Processor resources used to pack and unpack (for the most part for integer addition, multiplication and division).
2. Memory space required by the packing/unpacking routines (see section 2.8 for some cost-reduction techniques).

An order of magnitude of the execution times (in microseconds ($\mu$s) or millionths of a second) of the required instructions is shown in Table 2.4. The difference is considerable! Not only do computations cost much less on a large computer, but large computers often store large databases.

The conclusions are therefore:

1. The larger the computer, the more worthwhile the packing.
2. It is in the interest of the user to find out the cost of packing and unpacking on his actual machine; this can easily be achieved by developing and experimenting with appropriate routines.

### 2.7.2 Processing Time Economies When Sorting or Searching

The time required to access a disk is generally about 20 to 60 milliseconds (*sometimes 400 ms on a minicomputer using diskettes*). In a monoprogramming

20

**Table 2.4**

|  | Small computer | Large computer |
| --- | --- | --- |
| Addition | 50 | 1 |
| Multiplication | 120 | 3 |
| Division | 700 | 8 |

environment, this time is totally wasted; in a multiprogramming environment only a part of it is wasted. But whatever the environment, the computations associated with a disk access are relatively expensive, averaging from 1 to 10 ms. In addition, the execution of READ and WRITE statements costs 0.2 to 5 ms.

The savings that can be achieved through the use of packing include:

the number of disk accesses (since each access can bring in more data);
the memory space, if packed tables are used;
the amounts of data transferred between the disks and processor (packed data are less cumbersome);
the processing time: packed fields take less time to *compare* or *move* than longer, unpacked, fields.

### 2.7.2.1 Sorting Time Savings

The multiple base formula yields an $N$ which requires a space independent of the order of the packed fields. $N$ has $p$ digits; no matter how the computer actually stores and handles the integers, we can sometimes store the sort key fields as consecutive high-order digits. Comparing two records amounts to comparing their associated $Ns$. The $Ns$ require less space than their records do; it is faster to compare or exchange the $Ns$ than it is to compare or exchange the actual records.

When multiple-word packing is used, care must be exercised as the comparisons and exchanges may require access to several words; sorting is not practical when the sort keys are in different words.

### 2.7.2.2 Retrieval Time Savings

In a memory table, comparing packed data is faster than comparing longer, unpacked data. Therefore, when searching for a given piece of data, this can first be packed, then compared with the values in the packed data table.

### 2.7.3 What Fields Should Be Packed?

Generally speaking, packing should first be considered for all the data that are not very frequently accessed, as the processor packing/unpacking costs will then be small compared with the storage costs.

The groups of fields that make up sorting keys or search keys should be packed *separately*, that is in separate words. This will avoid packing or unpacking an entire record to process a few keys.

### 2.7.4 Secret Packing — Encryption

When multiple base packing is used, a given field cannot be associated with a group of bits, but a given bit can belong to several fields at the same time. For example, the low-order bit of each word changes from 0 to 1 each time the parity of the resulting $N$ of that word changes from even to odd; this may happen when *several* of the $N$ fields vary.

This is because:

the bases are not, in general, powers of 2, which alone would yield independent bit groups.

packing uses the $n$ bits of a word *jointly* in order to store the maximum ($2^n$) possible data combinations.

This characteristic can be used to achieve data secrecy. When the disk is read, no matter how the bits are interpreted (in decimal, hexadecimal, octal or binary form) one cannot set up a translation table. In each word, the value of $N$ results from the values of *all* the fields; The field values seem to conceal each other. The only conceivable deciphering method is the actual unpacking technique, which implies knowing the succession of the bases, and the technique itself. To effectively protect the data, the packing/unpacking routines must also be protected:

their source code must not be available;

their object code must be interspersed with unused data;

their access and use must require a feature like the dynamic password described in section 2.7.5 below.

The combination of the packing and dynamic password techniques results in very effective protection. The author has seen the *total loss* of a database that had become undecipherable following a sabotage; the database administrator who alone could assign new passwords and change the packing routines left the company after making unknown changes.

### 2.7.5 Dynamic Password

This password technique is used via a terminal. The computer displays on the terminal a long *random* number. The user calculates a password response to this number such as: multiply the third digit by the fifth, add the eighth digit, then add 0120 (the month and day). He types in this response. The computer analyses it and decides whether to accept it or not. The password is not a 'word'; it is a *rule*. If someone were to watch the response and try it when alone, the chances are that the random number has changed and access will be denied.

This technique is reasonably simple and safe. It also features the possibility of a *hierarchy of passwords*; if several correct responses are acceptable, the computer can determine what type of access it should grant following a given response.

22

## 2.8  HOW TO REDUCE THE COST OF DATA PACKING: USE OF BASES OF THE FORM $2^n$

A method called 'bit-packing' is aimed at reducing the processing cost associated with the packing technique discussed above (and which can by contrast be called 'numeric packing'). Bit-packing is a form of numeric packing which uses only bases of the form $2^n$: 2, 4, 8, 16, 32 . . . etc. The method is not applicable if the computer to be used does not have a bit-access capability.

### 2.8.1  Choosing the Bases

The method is the same as in sections 2.4, 2.5 and 2.6 above except that each base $B_i$ must be replaced with a base $B_i' \geqslant B_i$ where $B_i'$ is the smallest power of 2 which is at least as great as $B_i$. Each field is packed into a series of adjacent bits.

### 2.8.2  Packing and Unpacking

Packing and unpacking can be performed field by field instead of packing or unpacking the entire record. A field value can be 'written' into (or 'read' from) the appropriate bit positions using fast bit-manipulation instructions instead of arithmetic operations.

### 2.8.3  Advantages of This Method

A number of experiments performed on a medium-size computer have produced the following results:

1. The packing/unpacking speed using FORTRAN routines was with numeric packing: 150 microseconds ($\mu$s) per character; with bit-packing: 30 microseconds ($\mu$s) per character.
2. Bit-packing produced records equivalent or slightly less compact than numeric packing; in general, the difference was only about 10%.
3. The overall processor load using bit-packing was 30% *less* than with unpacked data, 40% less than with numerically packed data, during the execution of the database access or reorganization routines.

Bit-packing, however, does not preserve data security; it is far less difficult to build a translation table for each field of a record than with numeric packing.

# CHAPTER 3

# Disk File Structures

This chapter discusses an important aspect of database management techniques: storing data on disks.

In the previous chapters, we have seen that processing a database implies:

1. *Direct* access to the data: this in turn implies the use of disks or diskettes. From here on, we use the term 'disk' to designate diskpacks, fixed-head disks, drums, diskettes (floppy disks) and so on. All such devices are mass storage devices featuring random access.
2. The use of *physical* files containing data that satisfy as much as possible the three fundamental database definition criteria: exhaustivity, non-redundancy and structure.

We will discuss disk file structures with database management in mind. Thus we will concern ourselves with *permanent* files as opposed to *work* files (that have a useful life of a few minutes or hours). Similarly, we will not be interested in *transaction* files (used to carry data between two processing steps such as data capture and file update). And, of course, we will not cover *input/ouput* files (such as card images or printer records). The data of a database is by definition permanent, and temporary data does not have the same management-decision orientation and implications. Moreover, it is a mistake to handle temporary files with a database management system, as:

the structure of such files is simple (sequential or random access);
the cost of processing simple files with a database management system is three to ten times higher (in terms of CPU seconds and number of disk accesses) than the cost of processing with 'ordinary' file access techniques (sequential, random, indexed . . .).

We will discuss applications and file structures used in *business data processing*, as opposed to other areas such as documentation retrieval used in public libraries.


## 3.1 FUNDAMENTAL OPERATIONS USING A DATABASE

No matter what the purpose of a business database is, it is remarkable that the various processing (access) operations that are performed can always be expressed as a combination of one or several of eight fundamental operations, which we will define below. We will need accurate knowledge of these access operations to appreciate:

if a proposed file architecture is well suited to the intended application;
how complex the file management software will have to be, thus allowing for a correct comparison of various possible file structures.

We shall discover later that we need to be able to handle a database as easily as a deck of punched cards (we can visually locate a card, remove it from the deck, add a card to the deck inserting it in a chosen location, change its contents by punching specific fields). The capability and ease of handling require:

a clear understanding of the corresponding fundamental operations—the purpose of this section;
a description of the appropriate programming techniques—the purpose of the next chapter.

The eight fundamental operations can be subdivided into two classes:

1. The five data manipulation operations:
   'zero' or initial creation,
   ' + − ' or addition-subtraction,
   'MOD' or modification,
   'SEL' or selection,
   'RES' or restructuring;
2. The three data evolution operations:
   ' + → ' or linkage,
   ' + I' or index creation,
   ' + F' or field addition.

The five data manipulation operations are discussed below; the three data evolution operations will be covered in section 3.6—open content databases.


### 3.1.1 Initial Creation

This operation performs:

the initial physical file space allocation;
the creation of various pointers or counters (such as writing the first record—known as *header record*—of a file, with a pointer field that contains the address of the first record available for storage—record no. 2 in this case);
the loading of a table that contains some rules or data to guide all subsequent processing (such as the set of numeric bases used in the packing of the data records).

From here on we will use the symbols 'zero' or '0' to designate this operation.


### 3.1.2 Record Addition/Subtraction

This operation performs:

25

the creation (sometimes called 'insertion') of one new logical record in the database by 'adding' it to all existing records, and updating the associated tables, indexes, pointers;

the destruction (or removal, or deletion) of one existing logical record by 'subtracting' it from the set of existing records and updating the associated tables, indexes and pointers.

*Example 3.1* Add a new customer's record to the customer master file; subtract a cancelled order from the open order file.

Depending on the database management system, the subtraction may be *physical* (that is, the record space of deleted record is immediately made available for any subsequent addition) or *logical* (that is, the record to be deleted is flagged, but not erased or placed in a table (or chain) of available records; it will actually disappear during a future RESTRUCTURING operation).

The symbols ' + − ' or ' − + ' are used to identify this operation.

### 3.1.3 Individual Field Content Modification

This operation will change ('modify') the individual piece of data contained in a specific field of a given record. Note that this is an 'atomic' alteration; it concerns *one field of one record*, not an entire record (as + − does), or an entire file (as ZERO does).

This operation provides, on a disk database, the same flexibility we have on a card file; changing just one field of a record, no matter how small the field is. All fields can thus be modified—one by one—except *key* fields, used to identify logical records.

The ability to MODify field values will be quite useful:

to complete the loading of a database which had some 'empty' fields at the time it was created by + − ;
to update field values (such as a 'total sales' field of an item file record);
to recover from errors (bad input data, faulty handling or programming).

*Example 3.2* Consider an accounting database. Each account record contains four fields:

1.  the account number;
2.  the account name;
3.  the total monthly debit;
4.  the total monthly credit.

Suppose that, at the end of February we have monthly totals. A number of accounting operations take place in March. At the end of March, we replace the February monthly totals by March totals. To do that, we perform MOD operation(s) for each account record affected. Assuming that the MOD transactions come from a transaction file, we can sort the file by account number and field number, then run a sum-up program that replaces all individual MODifications concerning a given account and a given field by a global ('total') modification. We then perform the final MOD operations on the database, accessing each appropriate field only once, and each appropriate record once or twice only. This batch approach requires each MOD transaction to contain:

1. the record identification (the key in this example is obviously the account number);
2. the field identification ('3' or '4' in this example);
3. the new field value (new monthly total).

Let us now assume that a real-time update of the database is required. The various MOD transactions can be performed one by one, using the same format as above. However, in order to compute a new field value during a transaction, a program has to:

1. request a database 'read and retrieve with lock' operation for the given record;
2. compute new field value = old field value + transaction value;
3. request a database 'write and unlock' operation for the record.

(the 'lock' prevents *another* program (B) from attempting to update the record while the original program (A) performs phases (2) and (3), as this could result in a non-update for (B)).

### 3.1.3.1 First MOD Definition Extension

If we now define the new field value of the transaction format as (a, b) such that:

$x$ being the 'old field value',
$y$ being the 'new field value',
$y = ax + b,$

We achieve a more general, more powerful, more efficient MOD operation. The database management system must of course be equipped to compute such arithmetic expressions as $y = ax + b$, after reading field $x$ and receiving constants $a$ and $b$.

If $a = 0, y = b$ : this is a straight replacement of $x$ by $b$ as we just used;
if $b = 0, y = ax$ : this is a change of $x$ such as a 5% price rise ($a = 1.05$);
if $a = 1, y = x + b$ : this is a change of $x$ such as an inventory update (after selling three items, $b = -3, y = x - 3$).

This is more general and more powerful. In all cases, the three steps required previously to perform a MOD are replaced with just one step: request a database 'MOD'. This is more efficient for two reasons:

three database management systems 'calls' are replaced with one;
no locking is required (if the operation proves impossible, as would be the case for a negative stock, a failure code is returned together with the maximum allowable negative $b$ value, assuming $a = 1$). No-locking can be achieved if the database management system is 'uninterruptible' during an elementary MOD operation (in other words when it has started a MOD, it will finish it before it starts processing a transaction for another program).

27

### 3.1.3.2 Second MOD Definition Extension

Let us assume that we have to alter the 'quantity ordered' field of item number 4386 of the last order of customer number 56874. The logical data structure is a 'hierarchy' such as that shown in Fig. 3.1. (Each customer has 0,1 or $N$ orders linked to his record, each order header record has 1 or $N$ order item records linked to itself. This multilevel set of records with 1 to $N$ relationships is called hierarchy).

To perform the required alteration we must access the appropriate customer record, then follow the C → O linkage (which must be sorted in LAST IN, FIRST OUT (LIFO) order) to find his last order, then follow the O → I linkage, exploring all item order records until we find the record of item number 4386, then MODify the record's quantity ordered field.

The MOD format required is the same as in the previous example, except that the record identification is more complex; it is a *SELection* as defined below.

### 3.1.3.3 Third MOD Definition Extension

Let us assume that the new value of a field, $y$, depends on the previous value, $x$, and on the values of other fields belonging to the same record $R$ or to records $R_i$ accessed during the SELection used to find $R$. The MOD format required contains:

the format of the SELection used to find R;
the identification (name or number) of the field to be altered;
the alteration rule, of the forms $F_1$ or $F_2$:

$$F_1 : y \quad = a_1^1 x^1_1 + a_2^1 x^1_2 + \ldots$$
$$+ a^2_1 x^2_1 + a^2_2 x^2_2 + \ldots$$

$$\vdots \qquad \vdots \qquad \vdots \qquad \vdots$$

$$+ a^p_1 x^p_1 + a^p_2 x^p_2 \ldots + a^p_n x^p_n$$
$$+ ax + b$$

$$x^1_1, x^2_1, \ldots \text{ belong to } R_1$$

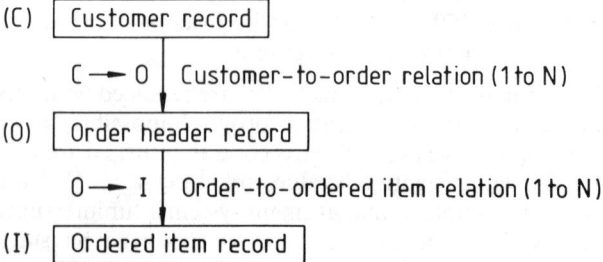

Fig. 3.1

28

$$x^1_2, x^2_2, \ldots \text{belong to } R_2$$

Where
$$x^1_n, x^2_n, \ldots \text{belong to } R_n$$

$x$ belongs to $R$

$$F_2 : y \quad = \text{IF } C_1 \text{ THEN } E_1 \text{ ELSE}$$
$$\text{IF } C_2 \text{ THEN } E_2 \text{ ELSE etc} \ldots$$

Where $C_1, C_2 \ldots$ are conditions similar to the conditions of a SELection and depend on fields of $R, R_1, R_2, \ldots R_n$, and $E_1, E_2, \ldots$ are arithmetic expressions similar to that of $F_1$

$$(y = a^1_1 x^1_1 + \ldots + a^p_n x^p_n + ax + b).$$

Note: $F_2$ is quite similar to the generalized assignment statements of high level languages such as ALGOL; such statements are easy to compile or interpret directly within the database management system or in a preprocessor program.

### 3.1.4 Data Selection (Retrieval)

#### 3.1.4.1 Primary Definition

We will call SELECTION (symbol: SEL) on a database the operation which extracts a subset of logical records which satisfy a number of specified criteria.

*Example 3.3* In a 'customer' database, select the customers of salesman SMITH who bought over $10 000 worth of shirts in November. In a 'personnel' database retrieve all that is known concerning employee 92743.
A SEL operation is defined by:

the criteria (sometimes called 'filters') used to select the subset of records;
the 'output file' (an actual file intended to receive the selected records, or the program that passed the SEL message to the database, a line printer, a CRT, etc.).

In addition, a *totalization* is often required. For example, the sales director (SMITH's manager) wishes to know the total year-to-date sales of those customers of SMITH who bought over $10 000 worth of shirts in November.
In short, following the primary definition, the SEL operation retrieves (for printing, displaying or storing in a work file) one specific record, a subset of the database or even the entire database.

#### 3.1.4.2 Secondary Definition

When the logical database record contains a considerable number of fields, it is often useless to extract an entire record. This is often the case especially in large and in open databases. It is more convenient, after retrieving records that satisfy

29

the criteria, to pass only a given subset of their fields to the 'output file'. The conventions below are followed:

the same subset of fields is extracted from each SELected record;
when the selected record does not contain a given field, the corresponding field output value is one that means 'absent' (a value that cannot be mistaken with an existing numeric or alphanumeric value).

When this mode of extraction (called 'selection with partial extraction') is used with an actual output disk file, a *standard format* should be used. For example, this standard selection output file' (SSOF) may have records with the following format:

12 numeric fields PICTURE S9 (13) V9 (4) (signed, 13 digits left and four digits right of the decimal point)
three alphanumeric fields PICTURE X(40) (40 bytes long).

The fields of *one* selected database record are stored in fields of *one* record of the SSOF. This SSOF may be sorted using a *standard* sort program (since its record layout is standard). After it has been sorted by customer number, an SSOF may be totalled using a *standard* summation program to calculate the total sales by customer. The output of the sort program is an SSOF, and is the output of the summation program. A *standard* statistics program can read an SSOF to produce histograms, various bar graphs, calculate means and standard deviations.

*Example 3.4* Consider a sales history database where invoices are stored; let us answer the following request: 'divide the customers among ten classes by total sales; for each class, provide:

the total sales of the class;
the number of customers of the class;
the cumulated sales of this and lower classes'.

This is carried out as follows.

1. We perform a SELection on the database, extracting invoice totals and corresponding customer numbers. Each selected invoice produces an SSOF record with two numeric fields used: invoice total and customer number.
2. This SSOF is sorted by customer number, producing a new SSOF (*standard* sort).
3. The new SSOF is summed by the standard summation program, generating an SSOF with only one record per customer (total sales, customer number).
4. The standard statistics program:
   reads the last SSOF one first time to find the minimum and maximum of the function 'total sales'; calculates the limits of the ten classes (dividing the interval into ten equal intervals);
   reads the SSOF a second time, storing each total sales field in a specific register and adding 1 to the associated counter;
   prints the requested results and the associated graphs.

Note: refer to Chapter 4 for more information about the SSOF and automatic reporting and statistics techniques.

### 3.1.4.3 Comments about Standard Selection Outputs

Standardizing the output format of a selection is only one aspect of a more general principle: *standardizing the format of the communication between a database and the application programs that access it.* This principle claims that it is important to standardize the formats of *all* fundamental operations, because *this makes application programs independent of database formats.* This independence implies that a given application program sends to (or receives from) the database only the data fields it actually has (or needs). It does not know that other fields exist. It does not concern itself with the actual formats of database storage (permanent) files. Consequently, if a permanent database file changes format, no application program is affected. If the sales history file had 18 fields in 1977 and three more fields are added in 1978 (bringing the total to 21 fields), all *existing* application programs that use the sales history file remain unchanged. This is quite important, as it dramatically *simplifies the maintenance of application programs that use a database.* It is so important that databases used to be defined as 'a collection of files with a structure and processor system (called database management systems) that provides program-data independence'. However, in the author's opinion, independence is a feature of interest to data processing personnel only. Exhaustivity, and non-redundancy, however, are of interest to all the users of the database. Independence may save an average of one compilation per day. Exhaustivity will be needed for 100 questions per day. That is why a database can exist without independence, but not without exhaustivity; and that is why the author's definition uses exhaustivity, non-redundancy and structure. A very successful database management system, IBM'S DL/1 does *not* feature independence, as it uses 'segments' to interface with application programs; this has not prevented several thousand computer sites from satisfactorily using DL/1.

In the late 1970s a new, enhanced form of independence has appeared, that between application programs and database *structures.* In this case, if the program uses a long access path to find the record to be processed, *it does not know the path in detail.* It does not know what file (or data set) is accessed first (and with what access technique, such as hash coding, indexing etc.), what inter-file linkage is used to access the second file, and so on. It only knows that the operation adds, subtracts, modifies or selects data. The actual path is supplied as *data* to the application program, for example by an 'operation catalog manager program'. Such a catalog is created and maintained by the database administrator. The programs obtain from the catalog manager completely pre-defined operation descriptions, and pass them to the database management system which *interprets* them. Sometimes a program updates a catalogued operation, supplying a customer number, for example, before it passes the operation to the database management system. With such a form of independence, application programmers do not need to know the database manipulation language; nor do they need to alter their programs if new data access or linkage paths are defined by the administrator; database management systems featuring such independence are the French SOCRATE, and the author's own RDS (Relational Database System).

### 3.1.5 Database Clean-up and Restructuring

This operation (symbol RES) will:

remove the subtracted or obsolete records, making their physical space available for addition;
make logically consecutive records physically consecutive;
verify the consistency of data links and pointers.

In other words, this operation leaves the database in the same state as it would have been after a number of additions (without subtraction) performed in the correct logical order.

*Example 3.5* Consider a customer payments file. Each record contains a header (customer number) and a series of subrecords, each of which represents an invoice and the associated payments.

The invoices which await payment are stored in the order of their invoice numbers; the header of each customer is linked (by a pointer) with the first invoice of that customer, and this in turn is linked to the second invoice, and so on. The restructuring operation will

1. remove the subrecords of fully paid invoices, leaving only the outstanding invoices;
2. remove the header records of customers who have no outstanding invoice left;
3. store all the invoices of a given customer in their logical order, linking the first to the customer header;
4. verify that all invoices do have a header, and that the associated customer number corresponds to an existing customer record.

Note that history databases are restructured by removing *obsolete* (too old) records (see section 3.2.1.2). In that case obsolescence generates the need for restructuring, not for subtraction.

### 3.1.6 Definition of Batch Processing, Transaction Processing, Real-Time Processing

The fundamental operations were defined in the previous sections by their action. It is also important to define their processing mode:

the time available to process the operation;
the number of records affected by each operation.

We now consider the following processing modes:

1. *Batch processing*, with processing times of several minutes or hours, and many records affected.

2. *Transaction processing*, which concerns one functional entity (such as one input order line) at a time. Note that a database may be used simultaneously in transactional mode for MOD and SEL and batch mode for +, − and RES; the processing times range from a second to several hours.

3. *Real-time processing* generally implies a transactional mode, and indicates that each transaction (or group of transactions) is processed *before* the next transaction arrives. This is the normal mode of operation with terminals. It implies sufficient processing power, and the ability to handle transaction stacks and waiting queues. In order to improve the *response time* (the time elapsed between the user action of sending the transaction and the arrival of a response to the user), it is advisable to reduce the waiting queues as much as possible.

## 3.2 CRITERIA FOR CHOOSING A STRUCTURE

The structure of a file is the result of a logical choice; we list below the main criteria for this choice.

### 3.2.1 The Type of Database

Commercial databases fall into three main categories:

the master file;
the history file;
the open item file.

Each record stored in a database is identified by a *key*; this key may (or may not) be located in the record, but its presence allows any two records to be identified and distinguished; logically speaking, two identical records cannot exist, although this situation could happen in a physical sense. The need for uniqueness, for + − and MOD operations, brings about the existence of a 'key'.

### 3.2.1.1 The Master File Type

This is the most frequently occurring type of database (see also section 3.3); in general, it is used mainly for its definitions (literals) and some key totals; it is most often accessed at the record level. For example:

the customer file (name, address...);
the item file (reference, literal...);
the stock (inventory) file (reference, quantity in stock...).

Operations on this file: additions ( + ) of records are rare, subtractions ( − ) are very rare. On the other hand, modifications (MOD) are more frequent. Key: customer number, item number, etc.

### 3.2.1.2 The History File Type

The history file (see also section 3.4) occurs less frequently than the master file; it is used as a record of all the useful details from certain types of transactions. It is built up on a 'stack' basis: the transaction records are stored in order as and when they arrive. For example, the billing history file where all the relevant details of each invoice are recorded—customer number, amount before tax, item numbers, quantities sold and the corresponding prices. The bills are dealt with in the order in which they are issued. The key is the invoice number.

Operations on this type of file: Additions ( + ) are frequent, subtractions ( − ) and modifications (MOD) are generally forbidden (since 'one cannot change history'). It is necessary to remove out-of-date records (archive) by a restructuring procedure (RES), where all records created before a certain date are erased.

### 3.2.1.3 The Open-item File Type

The open-item file (see also section 3.5) is used for keeping information of the logical record form:

Header → item 1 → item 2 → item 3 → etc.

For example, customer account file.
The structure of each logical record is:

Header: Customer name and address
item 1: 1st invoice number, amount invoiced, amount paid, means of payment;
item 2: 2nd invoice number, amount invoiced, amount paid, means of payment, etc.

#### 3.2.1.3.1 Operations on This File
Each logical record is created with its header and its first item; the other items are added as and when they arrive. Many additions and subtractions of items take place; when the last item of a header is erased, the header itself is also erased. Restructuring operations are frequent. We can see that the structure of the open-item file is more *general* than that of either the master file or the history file: it contains a 1 to N relation.

### 3.2.1.4 Complex Structures

Finally we will deal with structures of a very general nature, practically non-restrictive; we shall see how to build up at will the logical description of data items (in terms of quantity and size of fields), and how to integrate databases whose structures differ right from the beginning.

### 3.2.1.5 Comparison of Operations on the Three Main Types of Database

Table 3.1 compares operations on the three types of database. This is a rough comparison, intended only to highlight their differences.

**Table 3.1**

| Operation | Master file | History file | Open-item file |
|---|---|---|---|
| Addition method | By whole record, fixed number of fields | By whole record, variable number of fields | header, + 1st item, 2nd item |
| Modification permitted | yes | no | yes |
| Frequency of additions | rare | frequent | very frequent |
| Number of records added at one time | very few | average | average |
| Frequency of subtractions | very rare | never | frequent |
| Number of records subtracted at one time | very few | never | average |
| Frequency of 'clean-up' (restructuring) | very rare | extremely rare | frequent |

Note that the frequencies indicated correspond to the most standard form of batch processing. Real-time transactional processing sometimes produces much higher frequencies of low volume transactions.

### 3.2.2 The Amount of Data to be Stored

The most important criterion after the type of database is the quantity of data. Clearly, a structure—a method of organization suitable for database operations—is influenced by its size. When there are a few hundred records, a simple structure is good enough to ensure a good working efficiency; however, with a million records, we need a more elaborate structure to avoid wasting processing time.

Furthermore, the size of a file is the major factor that determines the type of media required; we can put a small file on a fixed-head disk—where the storage cost per character is high—whereas a large file can be stored on a removable disk pack, or a magnetic card store—where the storage costs (and the access performance) are low. The file structure takes account of the media used; it is often more time-consuming to change a disk pack or a magnetic card than to process a large number of records on the same disk pack or card; this leads us to the use of hierarchial index tables, etc.

Finally, an important consideration related to the quantity stored is the growth of a database. When the size may vary within a large range, the structure is adapted to this variation. For example; whether or not you allow for the situation where, after the stock is exhausted the list of back orders grows excessively in 1 month, will affect the adopted structure of the database.

35

### 3.2.3 The Processing Required

Once a database has been created, four types of operation are possible on it: +
−, MOD, SEL, RES. However, some of these operations will be more frequent
and/or will affect a larger amount of data and/or will be subject to execution
time constraints of varying importance. Clearly, in order to minimize execution
time, the structure must allow for these frequencies, amounts and time
constraints. In addition, some compromises are necessary; often disk space is
sacrificed in order to store several specialized index files when the execution time
for a search based on certain selection criteria (SEL) is of prime importance.

### 3.2.4 The Logical Structure of the Data

Certain databases contain what we will call 'single-level' data; an 'articles sold'
file, for example, has only one logical level, for the number of fields of a logical
record is constant. Other databases may contain 'two-level' data: for example, a
'billing history' file, where each invoice has a header and an undetermined
number of item lines. To consider such a file as single level reintroduces the
concept of *variable-length* records. Such records are always difficult to handle
on disk; we therefore use two physical files: the first for the invoice headers, the
second for the item lines. This permits, for example, specific interrogation
operations on the items, without reading or accessing the headers. We see in this
example that the logical structure of the data influences the physical structure of
the database (Fig. 3.2).

Note that the billing history file above is not a database of the open-item type,
as it is not suited to the numerous additions/subtractions of such a database; we
must, therefore, not confuse the database type and the number of levels it has,
or necessarily expect to find a relationship between the two concepts.

We strongly recommend the use of a written representation of the logical
structure, for example, in the form of a *tree* or a *level* description as in COBOL
or PL/1:

```
01 · · ·
     02 · · ·
     02 · · ·
                     occurs · · ·
        03 · · ·
        03 · · ·
     02 · · ·
```

before deciding on the structure of a database; we can thus avoid making regrettable decisions.

### 3.3 STRUCTURES FOR MASTER FILE DATABASES

This section considers file structures which are particularly suitable for the
'master file' type of database, whose essential characteristics are:

36

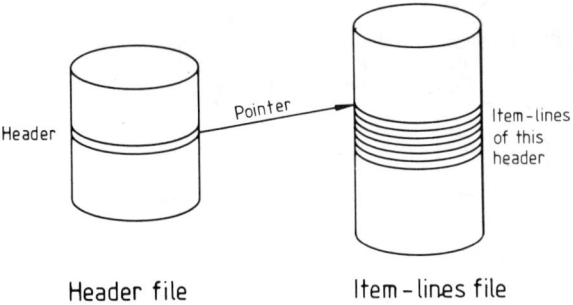

Header file           Item - lines file

Fig. 3.2

fairly high stability (additions/subtractions, modifications are fairly rare and/or of low volume, restructurings are unfrequent);

number of fields per logical record is constant

existence in each record of an 'indicator' field containing a value called a 'key', such that all the keys of the file are *different* (thus, for example, the key of a customer master file is the customer number. (All customer numbers are different: this allows us to retrieve them without ambiguity.)

However, these structures can sometimes be used for other types of database or for their 'index files' (defined below in section 3.3.2). Moreover, we frequently integrate two different databases, that is, we link them by pointers to allow the retrieval of the records of one base associated with certain records of the other. Thus, for example, during system start-up we can build up separately a 'customer' database (master file type) and a customer payments database (open-item type).

Each of these two databases (*actually sub-bases*) taken in isolation can be non-redundant; but considered as a whole, the corresponding files will have at least some duplicate customer numbers—we now have some redundancy; and if we subtract a customer number from the first database, we may forget to verify whether this customer is up to date with his payments, since the customer and customer payments databases are disjoint.

If, on the contrary, we integrate them by introducing pointers linking each customer with his payments chain, it is easy to verify that a customer is up to date with his payments before subtracting his entry from the customer database. This example (Fig. 3.3) illustrates the advantage of integrating databases and of non-redundancy.

Note: the table of 'payments' header has disappeared.

### 3.3.1 Sequential 'Stack'

This structure deals with records created in the most natural order for their creation, without considering their final means of use. It is therefore suitable only for small tables, not for databases as properly defined. We will not consider this structure for a master file type, but only for certain tables (header tables, for example).

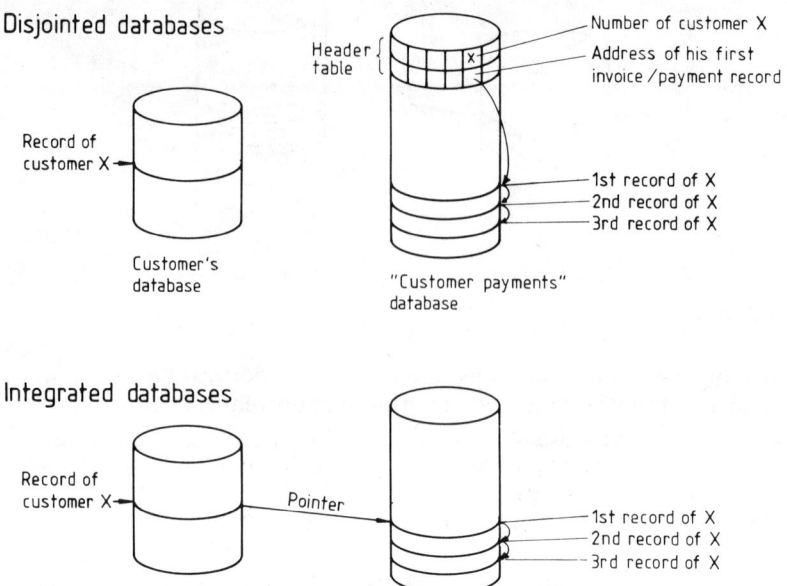

Fig. 3.3    Disjointed and integrated databases.

### 3.3.2 Sorted Sequential File: Index File

This structure deals with records created in the order most suited to the final use of the database.

#### 3.3.2.1 Operations

##### 3.3.2.1.1 '+'
The addition of a record after record $N$ involves the recopying of the file up to and including record $N$, then the writing of the new record, then the remaining records; the processing on disk is logically equivalent to that involved for magnetic tape; in particular, the records to be added must be presorted.

##### 3.3.2.1.2 '−'
The removal of a record can take place:

1.  *During* a record-addition operation (in this case we omit the recopying of the record to be deleted). Note that when we wish to greatly modify a record (by erasing it and adding it in its new form) we must do the subtraction *before* the addition: the sort for the + operations uses two keys. The primary key is the file key, the secondary key is the operation type: − comes before +

2.  *By 'logical deletion'*: we read the file up to the record to be deleted; we

then modify a field (the key field, for example) so as to indicate that the record is 'dead', and we then rewrite it. The record search can be done:

by sequential reading of all the records starting from the first;
by binary search (see Chapter 4, section 4.2) which is more suitable for large files;

Note that logical deletion is more suitable for large files, for it avoids the recopying of the whole file. In general, the low number of record deletions requires the presence in the addition–subtraction program of a special logical deletion sequence, intended for cases where there is no addition in the input transactions.

### 3.3.2.1.3 MOD
The modification of a record (designated by its key, the indication of the field to be modified and its new value) is made by locating the record (as above) and then recopying it in its new form. To minimize disk accesses and read/write operations within the same block, it is better to sort the input transactions on the file key.

### 3.3.2.1.4 RES
In principle, the restructuring of the file is senseless, since on each addition it is constantly sorted and useless records are removed.

### 3.3.2.1.5 SEL
The selection operation falls into two categories:

1. The selection criteria do not include the file key; each record must be read one by one to determine whether it is suitable (see section 3., 3.5.1)
2. The selection criteria do include the file key; when the criteria associated with the key are simple (for example, 'key > given number' or 'key = given value') the selection is faster because we can use a binary search and avoid having to read all of the records.

### 3.3.2.2 Remarks on This Structure

This structure has the advantage of being easy to understand and to put into operation. Furthermore, no disk space is required for the storage of auxiliary tables.

This structure has the disadvantage of requiring frequent recopies (+ − operations); it is therefore not suitable for databases with frequent additions or subtractions, or for real-time operations: *batch processing* or the *sorting* of transactions is required for this structure. We rarely use this structure for a database as defined, but it is often used for stable *index files*.

### 3.3.2.3 Definitions

We will call an index file (or 'directory') of a database, a file:

that has one record for each logical record of the database (one-to-one correspondence)

for which each record has two fields: the logical record key and a pointer that gives its address in the database (see Fig. 3.4).

The pointer may be absent; in this case, the address in the database is calculated from the record number in the index, either directly: database address = index record number, or at a constant displacement, representing the number of records in the database header: database address = record number + a constant.

The advantage of an index file is the *small size* of its records; for example, about 100 records can be read with a single disk access (100 records per block). Sequential reading thus allows rapid location of the desired key, if it exists. We can therefore access the database (in this case the access is based on *a given key*) by first searching the index (this is faster than searching the database from the point of view of disk accesses); then, with the help of the pointer or record number, we can access the database directly at the correct address.

If we frequently access the database using *several different keys*, *several indexes* are recommended, each based on a different key. This procedure has the inconvenience of creating a redundancy for each key, and therefore some precautions are necessary when using the operations + −, MOD and RES on the database; it will frequently be necessary to recreate the indexes. Fortunately an index file can be recopied rapidly (during updates) since it has small records.

### 3.3.3 Hierarchical Index

To speed up the search for a key in the index file, we can construct an index file for the index file itself. This 'higher level' index will contain only a single record for *N* records of the 'lower level' index file. We take *N* equal to the blocking

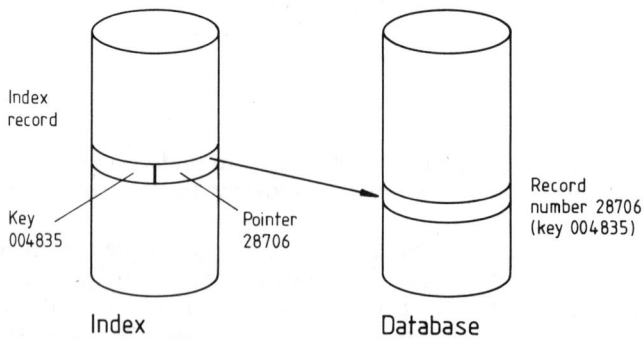

Fig. 3.4

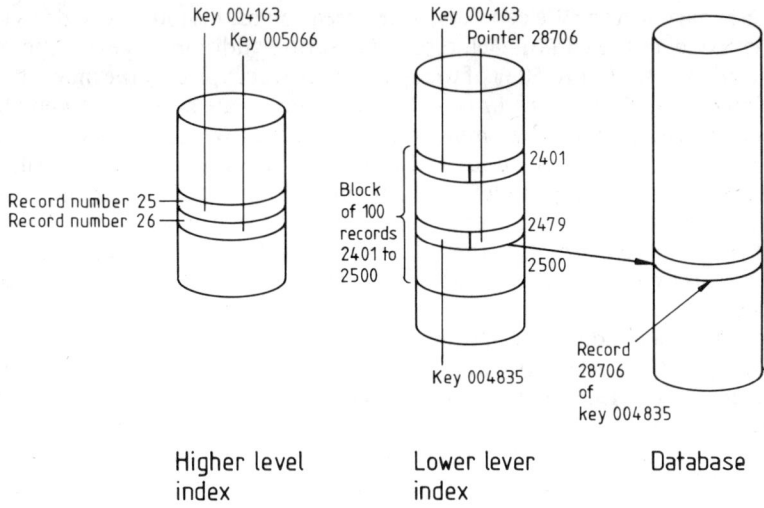

Key 004163
| Key 005066

Key 004163
| Pointer 28706

Record number 25
Record number 26

Block
of 100
records
2401 to
2500

2401

2479

2500

Key 004835

Record
28706
of
key 004835

Higher level
index

Lower lever
index

Database

Fig. 3.5    Search for key 004835: (1) In the higher level index: 4163 < 4885 < 5066 therefore 4835, if it exists, is in records 2401 to 2500. (2) In the lower level index: we find 4835 by binary search. (3) We then read the pointer 28706 to the database.

factor (number of records per block of the lower level index file), or to the number of blocks per cylinder of the disk pack, etc. The higher level index can be a separate file or can make up the header of the lower level index file. The higher level index is frequently fairly small in order to build up a table that we can keep *in memory* during the execution of the programs that access the database. This is made easier by the absence of a pointer and by methods of key packing (see Fig. 3.5).

We can if necessary build up a hierarchy of indexes, but this is generally limited to two or three levels.

### 3.3.4 Index with Partially Filled Blocks

A hierarchy of indexes has the enormous advantage of allowing rapid access to the records of a database. But, as with all sequentially sorted structures, the index must be reconstructed at each update. The recopying is not a problem for the higher level indexes, which are small by definition; only the lower level index is costly to recopy, as it has as many records as the database itself. However, the existence of the higher level indexes lessens the advantage, for all records *in the same block* of the lower level index, of sorting the lower level index; by and large it does not matter whether the records of a given block are sorted or not: the essential point is to be able to access this block with the minimum number of disk accesses. It is immaterial if, later, we must read sequentially instead of doing a binary search. We can thus, at the creation of this index, decide to leave 'a little space' at the end of each block, for future additions. We will therefore voluntarily waste 20% to 50% of the space on disk occupied by the index, but *we avoid 80% to 95% of the recopying*. Subtractions create holes in a given block. For each addition, after determining in which block we must place its record-key, we must scan the block until we find a hole. This hole can be the result of a subtraction, or can be space left free for this purpose, and can be used immediately for the new record. After a certain time, the first block becomes full; we must then begin to *restructure* the index; which involves the recreation of all the index hierarchy and the setting aside of new free spaces in the blocks of the lower level index.

Note: We can reduce the frequency of restructuring operations by setting aside some 'overflow blocks' for use when the original blocks become full. With this structure we need pointers at the end of each block and in the overflow blocks; the structure become more *complex* and its use on minicomputers is therefore not recommended. In general this degree of complexity is justified only for files that can increase in size very rapidly, and so suddenly that we cannot execute a restructuring operation in time. This situation arises frequently in system programming, but not in minicomputer application programming, and there solutions other than index files exist.

### 3.3.5 Indexed Structures

This structure—the most commonly found for a master file—consists of two logical files:

> the database file as such, whose records are stored in the order in which they were added;
> the *primary index* file (with one or two levels, each sorted in order to speed up access).

This structure sometimes also involves *secondary index* files. These are also sorted, but the fundamental property of the primary index need not be respected: the key need not be unique for records in the secondary index. Such keys have been built up from fields other than the key of the database, and thus the uniqueness of the key is not assured. Secondary indexes are therefore often at a single level, one index record per database record; in addition, the secondary index record often contains a single field, a pointer to the next database record (logically speaking), in the order of creation of the secondary index.

We may also come across secondary indexes whose records have two fields: the secondary index key and a pointer. The key is redundant, but its presence allows us to avoid reading the database for all key values to be ignored. The key can be the contents of a single field of the database file or several concatenated fields that we manipulate at the same time.

*Example 3.6* Let us consider a customer database whose primary index is based on the customer number. Suppose that the following processes must frequently be executed:

1.  Search for a customer (name, address, etc.) given his number.
2.  Search for all customers of a particular sales representative (whose code is given in the database, a single code for each customer).
3.  Print a listing of all the customers by department (the department code is a field in each customer record).

Process 1 uses the primary index. Process 2 uses a secondary index built up from the representative code; each record in the secondary index consists of the representative code and a pointer, sorted by representative code. Process 3 uses a secondary index consisting of pointers, indicating all the customers of department 01 (one record-pointer per customer), then all those of department 02, etc. (see Table 3.2)

### 3.3.5.1 Existence (Bit) Tables

Numerous applications exist where a certain number of selection criteria are privileged. Each of these criteria represents the presence or absence of data in a certain field (or less frequently, in a group of fields). For example, in a 'personnel' file with the following privileged criteria:

college education (yes/no);
more than 5 years' service (yes/no);
experience in manufacturing (yes/no);
commercial or marketing experience (yes/no);

each of the fields in question could contain more detailed information on the following points:

type of college studies, degree;
exact length of service;
previous positions held.

To simplify the searching, we then build an 'existence table' (sometimes called 'inverted' file) according to rules as shown in Table 3.2. Each field is represented by a bit with the convention that

0 = data absent
1 = data present

Each record of the database is associated with its group of descriptive bits by the relation 'same position'. Thus, for example, if we use four descriptive bits for each database record:

record 1 is associated with bits 1 to 4;
record 2 is associated with bits 5 to 8.

The existence table is stored in records of as great a length as possible (one per block, for example) in the header of the database file or in a separate file. A search for database records having certain characteristics is done by scanning the existence table. This search is rapid, as the table is not long. With computers that use bytes or half-bytes, it is better to represent a record as a multiple of these quantities.

**Table 3.2**

| Record number | Customer number | Representative number | Department number | |
|---|---|---|---|---|
| 1 | 001 | 17 | 06 | |
| 2 | 002 | 15 | 75 | |
| 3 | 004 | 06 | 59 | Customer |
| 4 | 005 | 17 | 08 | database |
| 5 | 006 | 06 | 62 | |
| 6 | 007 | 06 | 60 | |
| 7 | 009 | 20 | 91 | |

| Record number | Customer number | Pointer | |
|---|---|---|---|
| 1 | 001 | 1 | |
| 2 | 002 | 2 | |
| 3 | 004 | 3 | Primary index |
| 4 | 005 | 4 | |
| 5 | 006 | 5 | by 'customer number' |
| 6 | 007 | 6 | |
| 7 | 009 | 7 | |

| Record number | Representative number | Pointer | |
|---|---|---|---|
| 1 | 06 | 3 | |
| 2 | 06 | 5 | |
| 3 | 06 | 6 | |
| 4 | 15 | 2 | Secondary index |
| 5 | 17 | 1 | |
| 6 | 17 | 4 | by 'representative' |
| 7 | 20 | 7 | |

| Record number | Pointer | |
|---|---|---|
| 1 | 1 | |
| 2 | 4 | |
| 3 | 3 | |
| 4 | 6 | Secondary index |
| 5 | 5 | by 'department' |
| 6 | 2 | |
| 7 | 7 | |

*Example 3.7* Consider a database in a byte-oriented machine, where seven privileged fields have been defined, but where a whole byte has been reserved for each existence table record. Search for records whose fields satisfy the conditions:

| | |
|---|---|
| field 1 | : irrelevant |
| field 2 | : yes |
| field 3 | : yes |
| field 4 | : no |
| fields 5, 6, 7 | : irrelevant |

These conditions are equivalent to the following byte configuration

0 X 1 1 0 X X X

where the first 0 is for the bit not used, and the X's represent the irrelevant bits. If the machine features bit access, it is easy to generate a 'mask' which ignores the X bits and tests the state of other bits. If the machine does not feature bit access, the records to keep correspond to the bytes

0 0 1 1 0 X X X with value 30–37 (hexadecimal)
0 1 1 1 0 X X X with value 70–77 (hexadecimal).

More simply, if a byte represents two digits, we look for high order digits equal to three or seven and keep the corresponding records.

To give some idea of the speed of searching by existence tables: consider a database of 100 000 records where four privileged criteria have been retained, and suppose that the computer allows half-byte access. Each record is represented by a half-byte (four bits). Suppose that the existence table is stored in record-blocks of 5000 bytes; ten blocks are sufficient to describe the file. A complete scan of the file according to a combination of the four criteria therefore requires at most ten disk accesses to find the potentially useful records.

The ease of updating an existence table with + − and MOD operations should also be noted; the index does not have to be reconstructed—we only have to update the bits involved. Existence tables represent, therefore, a particularly useful form of index file.

Once we have accepted the usefulness of existence tables, we start to consider how we can overcome the limitation of the 1/0 or yes/no pair from the information it contains.

We can of course add to the binary information other information which can have more than two values, but this makes the table longer. It is possible, for example, to select all the fields which can make up selection criteria, and pack the data (to a base equal to a power of 2, or even to any base) and store the resulting number in an existence table. It is also possible to split the database itself into two parts:

the first part will contain information that is non-selectable or rarely selectable, or accessible by a separate index; this will be the major part by volume;
the second part, stored in another file, will contain in the most com-

pact from possible the data frequently selectable, and will at the same time make up its own existence table.

### 3.3.5.2 Operations on Indexed Structures

'+'. A new record is always added to the end of the file, after previous verification that it does not exist in the index. Updating of the primary index is done in two stages:

> during additions to the database, we note the keys and corresponding addresses in a work file; at the end of a batch of additions (or at the start of the next use of the file) we do a sort–merge, regrouping the index and the work file above, regenerating the higher level indexes where necessary.

'–'. Subtraction of a record is done by logical destruction (marking) in the index and/or the database. At the end of a batch of + – operations we update the index as above.

Note: We can see that the need to reconstruct or even simply update the index becomes costly if the number of + – operations increases; this structure is suitable only for files which are relatively stable with respect to the creation/destruction of records. To reduce this inconvenience we sometimes use indexes with partially filled blocks (Chapter 3, section 3.3.4). When the + – processing is done by batch, for example once a day, the relative cost (relative processing time) of reconstructing the index is of little importance. We can easily accommodate this, all the more so because the small size of the index records makes the sort rapid. But when the + – processing is done in transactional mode, with a very short time allocated for processing (a few tenths of a second per transaction, for example) we do not have time to update the index:

> subtractions are done by marking the database record only;
> additions are done in an overflow area (or overflow file) in the order of arrival;
> it is better before each transaction to search first for the key in the index proper, and, if we do not find it, in the overflow index;
> we must frequently update the index, incorporating the overflow index and sorting it (since transactions are blocked in batch mode).

'MOD'. Modification of a record is easy and poses no problems; it is always recommended to sort the modification transactions in order of the index key, to make accessing the index more rapid.

'RES'. Restructuring operations are always applied to the primary index; they take the database records in order of the primary index and recopy them.

'SEL'. Selection works in particular on an available index: that is, faster than a sequential scanning of a file.

*Notes on the physical structure of the primary index*
(a) The primary index can be stored:

> in the same file as the database itself (or one of its files) but this method is not very practical for sorting the index, particularly if it consists

of several hierarchical levels;

in a separate file, which we can easily sort, with the higher level indexes all regrouped in a second file (not sorted).

(b) The primary index must, in any case, be read rapidly. Now we know that the cost of a read depends on:

the number of disk accesses and reading instructions
the execution times of the above.

1. Construct an index hierarchy (with a maximum of three levels).
2. Group the key-pointer records in blocks containing the maximum number of records compatible with memory usage.
3. In order to reduce the number of reading instructions inside a given block, build records containing *several* key-pointer groups. These will be *read into a table* and we will search the table by binary search or 'improved binary search' of the keys (described below, chapter 4). We will thus avoid the time required for reading, which is much greater than that for transfers and comparions. Ideally, if the system permits, we should have a single record with several hundreds of key-pointers per block, read directly from disk into table (without passing through a buffer).

### 3.3.6 Indexed Sequential Structure

This structure is supported in various forms by many computer manufacturers, who include it in their system software. It is an indexed structure (see section 3.3.5) with the following characteristics: the database records are kept in their logical order (key order) by linking each one to the following one by a pointer (which gives it a 'sequential' character); when the actual database is created, or after every restructuring operation, about 20% to 30% of each block is left *empty*: this free space acts as an overflow area; we can add there any new records that are created, each one logically inserted between two records in the block. These records are linked by pointers from their predecessor and to their successor. Since each block contains an overflow area, the number of disk accesses is reduced for + − operations, at the cost of a 'waste' of disk space of the order of 20%; the index has one, two or three levels; at the highest level is a small table, generally available in memory, when the file is open; the lowest level is limited to a block of the database, whose first or sometimes last record it points to. In order to find another record in this block, we access it and read it in logical order: that of the pointers.

To find a free space in the block, we scan it in sequence, for example, until we find the first record that has been logically deleted or not yet used. The indexed sequential structure has only one advantage over an indexed structure; we can scan the whole database in its logical order (sequential) without reading the index. This advantage is not very important for a database, and we therefore tend not to use this structure often.

Note, however, that keeping the lowest level index to one record per database block and leaving some available space in each block is an alternative to the

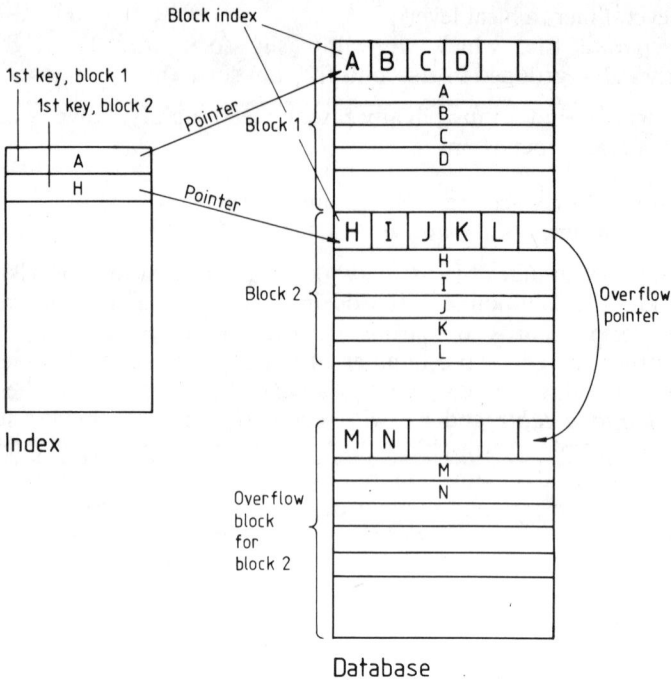

Fig. 3.6 Block index structure.

block overflow area technique. It also leads to less frequent restructuring of the index (but at the cost of greater wastage of disk). On the other hand, it allows a reduction in the number of keys in the lowest level index, and thus can sometimes save a level.

Alternatively, in order to reduce the search time for a record within a block, we sometimes use a 'block index' (Fig. 3.6); a record of the block (the first, for example) contains a table of keys for the records of the block. The scanning of this small table, which has as many entries as there are 'useful' records in the block, is much more rapid than a succession of reads, since the calculation time for a read into memory is not negligible, especially on small or medium-size computers.

### 3.3.7 Computed Address ('Hash Coding')

The structures most commonly used for master files are indexed structures. The index hierarchy allows access to the records in random order (this 'order without order' being the most frequently used for such a database). But there are two requirements for the use of index files:

reconstructing the indexes from time to time;

spending time (for disk accesses and reading instructions) in searching the

48

index files, even before accessing the information proper stored in the database.

These two requirements, which are costly in execution time, become more and more difficult to accept as the following two factors increase:

the size of the database file (number of records);
the access rate (number of searches or updates per unit of time), notably for teleprocessing.

We will therefore try to bypass the inconvenience of an index, by replacing the search in the index by a *direct calculation* of the address of the database record sought. This method of address calculation (hash coding) thus associates *an address* (a number) with a given *key*. For example, we can imagine searching for the address of a customer (whose key is composed of the first six characters of the name) by putting A = 1, B = 2, $\cdots$, Z = 26, then adding the values thus obtained to find the address. Thus, the customer 'COMSAT (CORP)', for example would have address $3 + 15 + 13 + 19 + 1 + 20 = 71$.

This process, however, has some inconveniences; what, for instance, would happen for customer 'SOMCAT'? Evidently, his record would also have to be stored at address 71, which is impossible! There are thus two cases to consider in address calculation:

1. Where the method of calculation ensures that only one possible key is associated with a given address.
2. Where a given address can correspond to several possible keys (we then speak of 'collisions').

Let us first examine two examples of the first case:

Example A: the key (numeric) constitutes the actual address
Example B: the key (alphanumeric) is limited, for example to the letters of positions 1, 2, 4, 6, 8, 10.

Example A implies that an eight-digit key points to a data base of 100 million records.
Example B implies $26^6$ records, or several hundred million.

We can see that databases will rarely have this structure, for the wastage of space would be enormous in most cases. The rest of this section, therefore, deals with the description of addressing methods in 'collision' structures.


*3.3.7.1 Addressing Algorithms for Numeric and Alphanumeric Keys*

According to the system and the file, the address to calculate can be a whole number or a group of numbers, identifying for example the disk unit number, the cylinder number, the track number, and the record within the track. Because of this, we nearly always give up the idea of doing a direct calculation of the address, since this involves several numbers; we first calculate the 'theoretical' address and then deduce the corresponding numbers of the physical address.

In the text below, we can suppose, to simplify matters, that the address is a *single number*. There are numerous methods of address calculation. This results from the fact that the keys to be transformed into addresses can have numerous possible structures:

their nature (alphabetic or numeric);
their length (number of characters or digits);
the semantic of their construction (idea represented by each character or group of digits or signs).

The variation is infinite. We give here only a few methods which are fairly easy to put into practice. Whatever the method used, it is better first to calculate the storage costs involved:

in calculating the number of possible addresses (and hence the number of records, and the overhead);
in calculating the rate of occupancy:

$$\frac{\text{space used}}{\text{total size of file}}$$

and assure ourselves that the costs are acceptable. Note that it is necessary to plan for a method of calculation which generates a number (A) of addresses higher than the number of possible keys (C). The higher the value A/C, the smaller the risk of collision, but the greater the wastage. In general, we try to make A/C < 2 if the address calculated is for the database itself, in order to limit the wastage. But if the address is for an index file, we can tolerate higher values, ten for example.

### 3.3.7.1.1 Methods for Alphanumeric Keys

These methods are used, for example, for *input without coding*.

*Example 3.8*   We need the customer name to input orders. We can type in the first ten characters of this (adding blanks at the right if necessary), without worrying about the customer number, which is, however, necessary for the actual processing. Suppose we have done this at a visual display terminal, connected to the computer. Input without coding has been used to avoid the operation of 'order preparation', which involves searching manually for the number associated with each customer and adding it to the order form. The operator types in the name (all letters), the computer looks for the number associated with the name, and then for the other details of the customer (address, etc.) and displays them on the screen. The operator checks these details against those on the order form; if they correspond, she types in the rest of the order, otherwise she checks the spelling of the customer name, and his number if necessary (against an alphabetic list) and starts again. If the machine finds an irregularity (such as, several customers with the same name, or the address calculated corresponds to several names) it displays all the details for each customer found, the operator chooses the 'correct' customer, and types in his number.

The method used takes into account six letters of the name and their respective positions. So, for example, we can use letters placed in positions

1, 2, 4, 6, 8, 10

associated with numbers by the method

$$A = 1, B = 2, \cdots, Z = 26, \text{blank} = \text{zero}, - = 27, ' = 28$$

We can multiply

the value of letter 10 by 1
the value of letter 8 by 2
the value of letter 6 by 3
the value of letter 4 by 5
the value of letter 2 by 7
the value of letter 1 by 11.

We multiply together the six values obtained and divide the result by the file size (number or records) which must be a prime number. We will add 1 to the remainder of this division, to give the address. For example, the name BARSAC will be transformed as follows:

| letter number | | | coefficient | |
|---|---|---|---|---|
| 1 | B = | 2 | 11 | $2 \times 11 = 22$ |
| 2 | A = | 1 | 7 | $1 \times 7 = 7$ |
| 4 | S = | 19 | 5 | $19 \times 5 = 95$ |
| 6 | C = | 3 | 3 | $3 \times 3 = 9$ |
| 8 | blank = | 0 | 2 | |
| 10 | blank = | 0 | 1 | |

$22 \times 7 \times 95 \times 9 = 131670.$

Suppose the file size is 9973 records (a prime number). We divide 131670 by 9973, giving a remainder of 2021. We add 1 to this value to obtain an address of 2022.

The methods for alphanumeric keys use the principles illustrated in the above example:

transformation of letters into digits;
choice of certain letters;
multiplication of number-letters by coefficients (base of the alphabet—28 above—or successive prime numbers);
multiplication of the results;
division by the file size;
addition of 1 to the remainder to find the address.

Note that most often the address will point to a file whose records contain only the ten letters of the alphabetic key, and the actual address of the whole record in the database. This type of index file inevitably leads to a wastage of space, due to the existence of addresses which will never be reached; but the wastage will involve *small* records, not the records of the database. We will see on the other hand (section 3.3.7.2 below) that this index file structure readily lends itself to the rapid elimination of duplicate keys.

### 3.3.7.1.2 Methods for Numeric Keys
These methods involve a transformation, which associates an address with a

numeric key. For the purposes of the description, we do not need to know whether the transformation produces an address in the index file or in the database. These questions of structure will be dealt with below. Let us simply note the following general point: the maximum number (A) of addresses resulting from the transformation must be higher than the maximum number (K) of keys, for certain addresses will never be reached. But even if the value A/K is higher than 1, we cannot, in general, determine the number of collisions resulting from a transformation; consequently, we recommend the following experimental steps:

1.  Construct a file 'F' containing all the keys (take the database itself if it already exists elsewhere with another structure).

    In the case of large databases (with greater than 10 000 keys, for example) we can make do with a *sample* of all the keys. But this sample must be fairly big, to make it as representative as possible, and must include all the possible cases of codes forming a particular key—with the same frequency of occurrence.

*Example 3.9*  Consider a customer file with 100 000 records, 80% of which concerns customers of type 'A' and 20% of which concerns customers of type 'B'. The type corresponds to the first digit of the key. We can take a sample of 10 000 customers, 8000 of type A and 2000 of type B. For each one, we can punch the key on a separate card; these cards make up the file 'F'.

2.  Write a small program where we can insert successively the different transformation formulas to evaluate. This program scans the whole file, calculating the address associated with each key, and noting this in a file (S). A record of S contains two fields: the address obtained, and the key used.
3.  Sort the file (S) on the address obtained.
4.  List the sorted file; collisions can arise in the form of consecutive records with the same address.
5.  Using a second small program which reads the sorted file (S), determine:
        the number of unused addresses,
        the number of addresses corresponding to a single key,
        the number of addresses corresponding to two keys,
        the number of addresses corresponding to three keys, etc.
6.  Compare the above results for all the different candidate transformations. Choose the transformation which produces the best compromise between wastage of space and number of collisions.

*Extraction of a reduced key.*  A key sometimes contains several parts.

*Example 3.10*  The key (eight digits) is an item number and is built up of three parts:

the item type (four digits);
the size (two digits);
the colour (two digits).

The fourth digit of the item number is most often 0: we will not use it in the transformation. In addition, the first digit of the size is most often 4; we will not use it either. We can therefore extract from the key a *reduced* key from the digits 1-2-3-6-7-8. The extraction method therefore involves using only the most significant parts of the key. We then apply one of the transformations described above to the reduced key.

*Division of the key.* This transformation begins with choosing the number of addresses (A) (greater than the maximum number of keys (K)). For each value $X$ of the key, we divide $X$ by A ('integer' division) and add 1 to the remainder R. The number R + 1 thus obtained is the required address. Remember that A must be a prime number.

*Multiple-base coding.* When a key consists of several parts (where, if necessary, only the most significant parts have been kept, in order to produce a reduced key) *we construct a table for each remaining part of the key.* Each table associates with each possible value for the corresponding part of the key a number-code: $0, 1, 2, \cdots, n$ ($n + 1$ is therefore the number of possibles values). We can then consider that we have a multiple-base coding for the key. Each part of the key can be represented by a unique digit in a base equal to the number $n + 1$ of values in its table. We can thus calculate the number $N$ of the *multiple-base formula.* The product of the bases gives a number A. If this number is not too big and if it gives an acceptable file size, we can take $N + 1$ as the address. *In this case hash coding is a transformation without collision.*

Notes:
1. In practice this transformation can be applied only if it leads to small tables, which we can easily store in memory.
2. To reduce the number A as much as possible, we must try to eliminate combinations of number-codes which cannot exist. This often results in regrouping some parts of the key and in increasing the size of the tables: a compromise is then necessary between the table size and the size of A.

If the product of the bases (A) is too big:
1. We can complete the transformation by dividing $N$ by A' $<$ A which we want to keep, and then add 1 to the remainder to obtain the address.
2. We can equally well multiply together all the number-codes extracted from the tables before applying the transformation by division. This second process results in the same number A (no reduction in the theoretical size) but the calculations are faster for they involve the formula

$$N = n_1 * n_2 * \cdots * n_p + 1$$

instead of

$$N = n_1 + B_1 * n_2 + \cdots + B_1 * \cdots + B_p - 1 * n_p + 1$$
(formula of multiple bases)

which saves $p - 1$ additions (where $p$ is the number of tables and bases). On the other hand we risk having more collisions; this becomes clear if we take the values of $N$ corresponding to

$$n_1 = 3 \qquad n_2 = 6 \tag{1}$$

then

$$n_1 = 6 \qquad n_2 = 3; \tag{2}$$

the values are equal. Of course with this second procedure we must start our coding with 1 instead of 0 as in multiple bases, or we may even remove the tables—the parts of the key are then multiplied together; this is a variation of the reduced key method of the transformation by division.

3. We can multiply the number in uncoded form, as extracted from the key, by constants (as in the transformation for alphanumeric keys, section 3.3.7.1.1) before applying a transformation by division.

### 3.3.7.2 Structures Suitable for Hash Coding

In describing the hash coding method, we have shown the necessity for a compromise in the following two aspects:

reduction in the number of collisions,
reduction in the wastage of space.

We must add two further constraints which are at the very origin of the choice of a hash coding structure:

reduction in the number of disk accesses necessary to access a record;
reduction in the amount of processing required for index reconstruction.

We can regroup these four constraints into:

a constraint on the amount of storage,
a constraint on the amount of processing.

From these last two constraints we can deduce whether to use a hash coding structure, and whether an index will be required in respect of the address calculation and the wastage of space.

#### 3.3.7.2.1 Use of an Indexed Structure
We use an index structure when the number of keys is small ( < 10 000, roughly speaking) and when the frequency of additions/subtractions is small (for example, a single index reconstruction per day, in batch mode). We also use this structure when we need to search through the database using only the beginning of the key (the first two letters for example).

#### 3.3.7.2.2 Use of a Hash Coding Structure without an Index
When we have to reconstruct the index several times per day on account of the frequency of additions/subtractions, and/or when we must have an index with three hierarchical levels on account of the number of keys, we use a hash coding structure without an index. We then have to find a key transformation which results in an acceptable wastage of space. This is often difficult, but when we have succeeded, we have two solutions for dealing with the problem of duplicates:

1. When there are few collisions (for example no collisions for 90% of the accesses) and there are not too many duplicates (two or three except in rare cases) we use a unique overflow area, situated at the end of the file (or in any position not accessible by hash coding). The duplicates are linked to each other by pointers: the structure is called 'end-of-file over-

flow chain' (Fig. 3.7). For this structure we must have *few* records per block, in order to diminish the volume of transfers on each transaction.

2. When the number of duplicates by collision, and/or the number of collisions, and/or the frequency of updates increases, we reduce the number of disk accesses required using chains of pointers and allowing *an overflow area in each block*: the structure is called 'end-of-block chain', or bucket block (Fig. 3.8). It involves a greater wastage of space than the end-of-file overflow chain structure. In addition, to allow for possible overflow of bucket-blocks, we must also set aside a 'general' overflow area at the end of the file.

For this structure we need to have blocks with a *large* number of records; because of this, the increase in performance with respect to the previous structure is noticeable only for systems whose disk channel transfer rate (number of

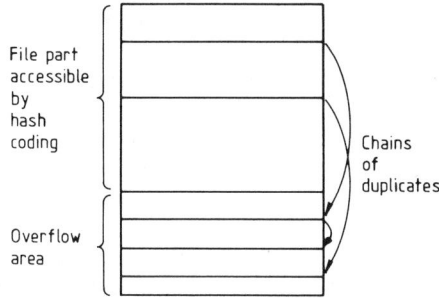

Fig. 3.7　End-of-file overflow chain structure.

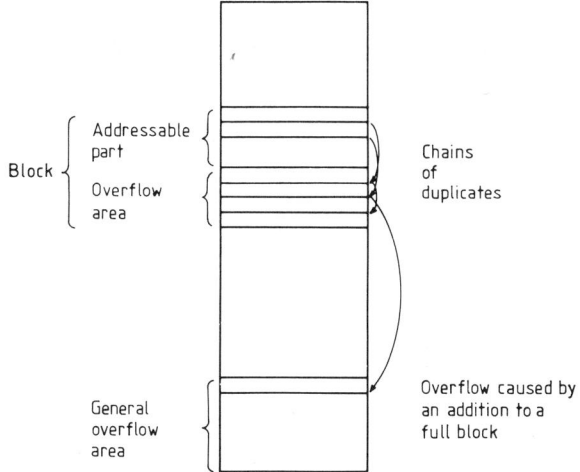

Fig. 3.8　End-of-block overflow structure.

characters transferred per second) is great. In addition, the blocks take up a lot of space in memory. Since wastage of disk space is great, the method is suitable only for powerful machines and 'real-time' applications.

Note: replacing the 'overflow area' technique with the 'adjacent block' technique.

The use of a general overflow area is not mandatory. When a bucket-block overflows, the necessary additional key space can be sought in adjacent blocks, up to a certain distance (expressed as a number of blocks). For example, if block 2612 overflows, we will try to insert the key in block 2613. If this is also full, we will try 2614 and so on.

Assuming that the maximum allowed 'distance' is $M = 100$, we will try all blocks up to and including 2712. If no empty space has been found, we will give up the addition and report a 'no-file-space' condition. At the end of the file, the 'successor' of the last block is (of course) the first block. This technique has the advantage of 'spreading out' collision areas. However, it requires a 'maximum overflow pointer' to be maintained in each block, to indicate how far it overflowed; otherwise, each unsuccessful search could require $M + 1$ disk accesses.

### 3.3.7.2.3 Use of a Hash Coding Structure with an Index

When the number of records in the file becomes considerable, the resulting wastage of disk space with direct addressing of a database is no longer acceptable. We then try to obtain better use of disk space at the expense of the performance associated with direct addressing, in transferring the wastage to the small records of an index file.

The use of an index file—which is less costly to read than a database file since its records are smaller—allows us, in addition, to reduce the access time involved in finding a given record when there are duplicates and when several reads are necessary.

The reasoning and conclusions formulated for the previous methods apply also to the index file: when the frequency of additions/subtractions and the number of collisions are fairly small, a general overflow area will be used; in the opposite case, an overflow area in each block will also be used (Fig. 3.9).

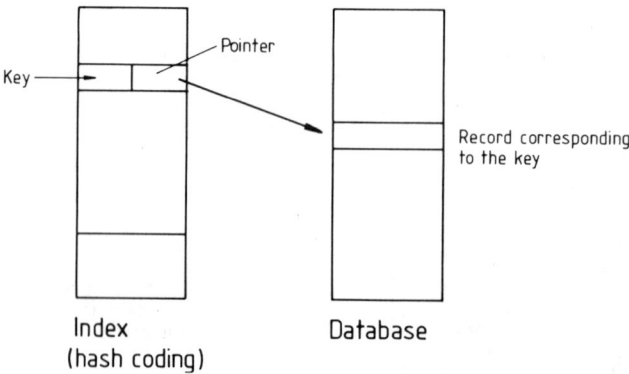

Index
(hash coding)

Database

Fig. 3.9

### 3.3.7.3 Fundamental Operations on Databases with Hash Coding

#### 3.3.7.3.1 '+'
Addition of a record involves the following stages:

1. Address calculation (according to the structure: index or database directly)
2. Verification of collisions:
   at the address level (another key stored at this address),
   at the key level (record to be created already exists).
3. Storing of new record in the database and eventually in the index. No index reorganisation on reconstruction.

#### 3.3.7.3.2 '−'
Deletion of a record involves the same stages, except that the records found are deleted by marking.

#### 3.3.7.3.3 'RES'
There is no restructuring. We can, however, after a certain time of use, consider reviewing the block size and the size of the overflow areas, and possibly change them.

#### 3.3.7.3.4 'SEL' and 'MOD'
Access by key is straightforward. But since there is no 'key order', there is no advantage in presorting the 'MOD' transactions (this is the opposite of indexed structures which undergo restructuring operations). On the other hand, we may want to sort selected subgroups by order of key.

### 3.3.8 How to Choose a Master File Structure

Generally speaking, the choice of a structure is made by initially picking out the possible structure models, then by calculating the characteristics of each model (size, number of disk accesses for each operation, etc.), and finally by comparing the results.

The following sections summarize the steps to be taken.

#### 3.3.8.1 File Types

Ensure, with the help of Table 3.1 (page 00), that the file in question is in fact of the master file type. Note that the most typical characteristics of a master file are:

  fixed length records, well defined by fixed contents and accessed in their entirety; most often accessed randomly, by key; stability.

#### 3.3.8.2 File Sizes

Establish carefully a list of the logical fields of a record, with their types (numeric, alphabetic) and their sizes.

Make allowances as far as possible for fields to be added at a later stage (type, number, size, etc.).

Determine the existing, future and maximum number of records.

Calculate the existing and maximum amount of space to set aside for the storage of data; do not take into account pointers, or headers.

### 3.3.8.3 Operations

For each basic repetitive operation ($+$ $-$, MOD, SEL, RES) determine:

the average number of records affected;

the frequency of occurrence of the operations (how many times per day, month, etc. these records must be processed);

the response-time constraints, if any (how much time is available for processing the specified records, a few hours by batch processing or a few seconds by transactional or even real-time processing);

the processing environment: monoprogramming or multiprogramming. Disk accesses produce delays in a monoprogramming environment, and may therefore seem costly; in a multiprogramming environment— especially when several independent disk channels are available—disk access time is made up for by other work. This situation often produces different database structure choices (for the same problem) according to the environment: we are more likely to concentrate on performance in a monoprogramming environment than in a multiprogramming one. Since minicomputers generally run under monoprogramming, it is more difficult—though more important—to devise an effective system for them. Large computers are extremely versatile, very fast, and possess powerful software (system and languages); as a result, design errors are more easily condoned. Despite what some people believe it is more difficult to program a small machine than a large one, but more difficult to organize the workload on a large machine than on a small one (due to the very fact that they use multiprogramming);

the important selection criteria may sometimes require the creation of secondary indexes;

the processing mode: batch, transactional, real-time. We can establish, for example, whether or not there is sufficient time for rebuilding an index;

the possible access conflicts. By an *access conflict* we mean the situation where two programs access the same file at the same time. Supervisors vary considerably, as to what access they will allow; some categorically forbid multiple accesses to a file, others only allow multiple reads, still others allow simultaneous reads and writes, but only to different blocks, whereas some allow simultaneous access of any kind. We will concentrate at this level on *visible* conflicts: do we want several operations on this file (corresponding to several terminals, for example) to take place at the same time, how often a day, with what maximum wait?

safety restrictions: constraints with respect to recovery time after an incident;

access security restrictions from a secrecy point of view.

The section above represents those specifications of the database which influence its structure. Below we describe the general work methods recommended for databases; here we will make do with a brief treatment of the problems involved in choosing a master file structure. This choice can be said to be the most important work after the specifications are built up, for a badly chosen structure can lead to excessive processing costs, prohibitive storage costs, or unacceptable response times.

In fact, for a master file, we can choose between two types of structure:

an indexed structure,
a hash code structure.

The choice between these two types is made as described in section 3.3.7.2, considering the number of records of the database, the processing mode and the time available for reconstructing the index. (See also the note on page 00).

If we choose a hash coding structure, we must decide whether or not to use an index. We first make a study of the possible transformations (see sections 3.3.7.1.1 and 3.3.7.1.2) and according to the number of collisions we can then decide

1. if there is so much wastage of space, that an index is required; and
2. if overflow areas are necessary both at the block level and at the end of the file, or only at the end of the file.

If we choose an indexed structure, we must first determine 'the critical operation': The most critical of all the operations ( + −, MOD, different selections, RES) is that whose volume and frequency of occurrence (in batch processing) and response time (in real-time processing) requires the most costly processing, or is the most difficult to carry out in the given time. Thus, it can happen that some databases (said to be 'very stable') require only a few + − operations but many SEL operations (the time required to reconstruct the index is then of hardly any importance). We can make do by assuring rapid selections using an appropriate structure. This is the case for example with most of the 'item' files of users who are actually the manufacturers of these items, on account of the stability of the range of products built.

If on the contrary a database is 'relatively unstable', and the number of + − operations is more appreciable, the time required to reconstruct the index is no longer negligible. We will use an indexed hash code structure with suitable overflow areas (this is used particularly for certain 'customer' and 'item' files).

Finally, if the database is obviously 'unstable', and the number of + − operations is high (for example 30% of records are created/deleted per day) we often return (paradoxically) to the structures for very stable files; we prefer to reconstruct a hierarchy of indexes, after restructuring the database itself after each daily + − operation. This is the case, for example, with the item files of wholesale dealers in food products, as these users modify their prices frequently.

After determining the critical operation, we choose the *type of lower level index* (if any):

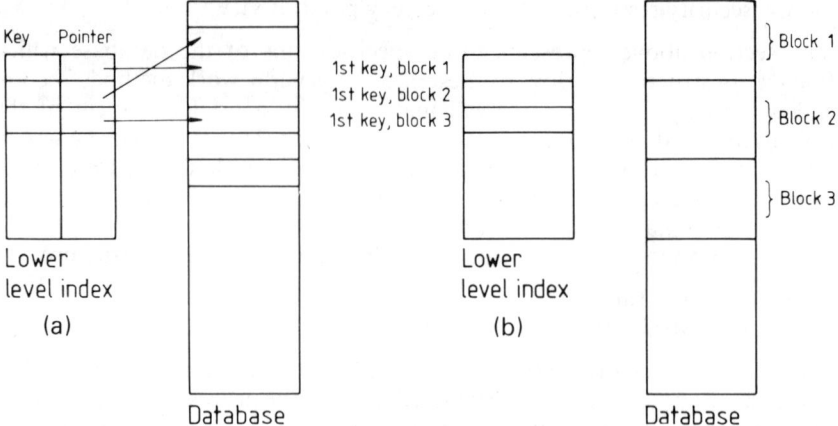

Key     Pointer

1st key, block 1
1st key, block 2
1st key, block 3

Block 1

Block 2

Block 3

Lower
level index

(a)

Lower
level index

(b)

Database

Database

Fig. 3.10   (a) Record-oriented index: each record in the database has its key and its pointer in the index. (b) Block-oriented index: only the first (or last) record in each block of the database has its key in the index.

    index per record, where each record key appears, generally with its pointer;
    index per block, where only the key for the first (or last) record of each block
       of the database appears; the implicit pointer results from the fact that the
       position of this key in the index and the position of the block in the data-
       base are identical (Fig. 3.10).

Very stable or clearly unstable master files generally have the most to gain from the use of a block-oriented index. There is then either no overflow area, or one at the end of the database file, where full blocks point to their overflow block by means of an appropriate pointer. When the blocks contain more than three or four records, it is better to use a 'block index' (see section 3.3.6 for more details).

The choice of a block-oriented index structure is justified only if it permits us to save an index level as compared with a record-oriented index structure. Since this varies according to the maximum size of block used, we should therefore verify this saving before making a final decision. In addition, a block-oriented index structure is more complicated to put into operation from a programming point of view if we set aside overflow blocks and indexes for the blocks.

Relatively stable master files generally gain from the use of a record-oriented index. According to the stability, we will use either overflow areas at the end of the file (most often) or overflow areas in each block of the index *and* at the end of the file (more rarely).

After choosing the type of index, we must determine the number of hierarchical levels of the indexes; for that we use the given maximum block size as a base, and also the maximum predictable number of records in the database. We first determine the number of logical 'key pointer' records per block of the lower level index (if possible a single physical record built from a table containing all the keys and pointers of the block; if not, one physical record per logical record).

60

We then determine the number of blocks and verify if, using one key per block, a block-oriented index of the lower level index can be contained in one single block. If so, we may restrict ourselves to two hierarchical levels for the index. If not, a third level is required. We then verify the structure thus determined by calculating the number of disk accesses corresponding to non-critical operations; if this number is acceptable, the structure is suitable, if not, we must try another structure giving a better compromise for the requirements of the different operations.

To finish off the choice of structure, we consider the header part of the database, which contains general information such as:

date and time of the last update;
number of records written;
available overflow addresses;
totals (paying attention to the question of redundancy);
the secondary index files.

### 3.3.9 Examples of Customer File Structure

To illustrate the method outlined in the above sections, we can now study the structure of a customer file, considering the cases shown in Table 3.3.

**Table 3.3**

| Case | Number of customers | Environment | Number of + − per day | Number of SEL per day (including statistics) |
|------|---------------------|-------------|----------------------|----------------------------------------------|
| 1 | 5 000 | Monoprogramming (batch processing) | 10 | 10 000 |
| 2 | 50 000 | Multiprogramming (batch processing) | 100 | 100 000 |
| 3 | 500 000 | Multiprogramming (terminal queries, + − in batch) | 5000 | 1 000 000 |

A customer record consists of:

a four-byte key,
a main record of 200 bytes,
in some cases supplementary records of 100 bytes giving delivery addresses, bill addresses, etc.

There may be, 0, 1, 2, or 3 supplementary addresses for each main record. Most often there is no supplementary address (80% of cases). Let us suppose that the maximum reasonable block size is:

case 1: 500 bytes,
case 2 and 3: 2000 bytes,

and that each pointer requires two bytes (for case 1) and three bytes (for cases 2 and 3).

### 3.3.9.1 Is the File a Master File?

As far as the record (stability, fixed-length, accessed in its entirety, most often by random access) is concerned, the file is certainly a master file type. Because of the supplementary addresses, we could consider it as being an 'open-item' type (see page 00). In fact, there are few modifications or additions/subtractions on the supplementary addresses; we will therefore set aside two physical files:

> a main file, containing 0, 1, 2, or 3 pointers towards possible supplementary addresses.
> an auxiliary file, reserved for the supplementary addresses.

This structure allows us both to economize on disk space—so we will not reserve 200 + 3 × 100 = 500 bytes for each customer record—and to map the logical structure onto a fixed structure, and therefore the database type to a master file type.

Note: an obvious alternative is to use random—access variable-length records, if such a file structure is available, and if its access performance is acceptable.

### 3.3.9.2 File Size

Assuming we have the maximum number of customers, and that the 20% of customers with supplementary addresses have, on average, 1.5 per customer, the maximum file sizes are shown in Table 3.4.

**Table 3.4**

| Case | Size of main file (M bytes) | Size of auxiliary file (M bytes) | Total file size (M bytes) |
|------|------|------|------|
| 1 | 1 | 0.15 | 1.15 |
| 2 | 10 | 1.5 | 11.5 |
| 3 | 100 | 15 | 115 |

We notice that in case 3 we have to use disk-packs of large capacity or set aside a multivolume file.

### 3.3.9.3 Choice between Indexed Structure and Hash Code Structure

Note firstly that additions and subtractions can be done once per day, in batch-processing mode.

### 3.3.9.3.1 Case 1
A small number of customers gives high stability: we choose an indexed structure.

### 3.3.9.3.2 Case 2

A fairly large number of customers still gives high stability; so the decision is more difficult. Let us evaluate the number of levels of index necessary if an indexed structure is to be used:

1 customer key (4 bytes) + 1 pointer (3 bytes) = 7 bytes.

We will therefore not use more than 2000 divided by 7, or 285 key-pointers per block in the lowest index level if we take a record-oriented index; we will not use more than 2000 divided by 4, or 500 keys if we take a block-oriented index.

In these two cases, a higher level index is required. This index points to the blocks of the lower level index. There are respectively:

$$50\ 000/285 = 175 \text{ keys or } 175 \times 4 = 700 \text{ bytes}$$

and

$$50\ 000/(N \times 500) = 100 \text{ keys}/N$$

(where $N$ is the number of records per block in the database).

In each case the higher level index fits into a single block, and therefore requires only one initial disk access in order to be loaded into memory each time it is processed. Therefore with an indexed structure, a customer record may be accessed using two disk accesses by SEL: (one for the lower-level index, one for the database).

Note: another advantage of indexes is the ability to search on 'partial' keys.

*Example 3.11* A customer file is indexed by *customer name*. Assuming that we want to retrieve a customer whose name begins with 'BIR', we can find the first key greater than or equal to 'BIR' and thus retrieve in succession: BIRCH, BIRD, BIRNENBAUM, etc.

In comparison, hash coding demands a complete, accurate knowledge of the key. It allows a reduction in the number of disk accesses by SEL from 2 to 1.1 or 1.2 at best, which is not very significant in batch processing with multiprogramming; and it requires a study of the transformations from a key into an address, and then more difficult programming.

We can therefore retain an indexed structure.

### 3.3.9.3.3 Case 3

A very large number of customers gives less stability. By similar reasoning to that for case 2, we see that the index hierarchy should have three levels, so therefore an indexed structure would require three disk accesses by SEL. On the other hand, a hash-coding structure with an index (on account of the file size) would reduce the number of disks accesses to two, which is important in reducing the response time during file interrogation from a terminal. In addition, processing for updates would be considerably faster due to the fact that we would not have to update or reconstruct the index, and restructuring operations could be omitted; we will therefore retain a hash coding structure with an index.

### 3.3.9.4 *Detailed Study of Structures*

**Table 3.5**

|  | Number of key-pointer pairs | Number of blocks in lower level index | Number of blocks in higher level index |
|---|---|---|---|
| Block index | 2500 (as there are 2500 blocks) | 50 (2500/50) | 1 (for 50 × 4 = 200 bytes, which is less than 500 bytes) |
| Record index | 5000 (as there are 5000 records) | 100 (5000/50) | 1 (for 100 × 4 = 400 bytes, which is less than 500 bytes) |

*3.3.9.4.1 Case 1*

This concerns a very stable database, resident on a small computer. We can now calculate in turn the characteristics of the indexes necessary in the following two situations:

> block-oriented index,
> record-oriented index,

knowing that a key-pointer combination occupies $4 + 2 = 6$ bytes, and that the maximum block size is 500 bytes; one block can therefore contain 500 divided by $6 = 83$ key-pointer pairs. We will suppose that block sizes of 300 to 400 bytes are acceptable (taking into account the physical size of disk segments), and will decide to use blocks of 50 key-pointer pairs in the index, that is to say, $50 × 6 = 300$ bytes, and group the records of 200 bytes in two's in each block of the database.

We can see from Table 3.5 that the critical operation (selection) requires the same number of disk accesses for the two types of structure; we will therefore choose a record-oriented index, which is simpler to handle from a programming point of view.

In addition, and again to simplify the programming involved, we will not use any overflow area other than that which is automatically reserved at the end of the database file. After each $+ -$ operation we will make do with

> recopying the lower level index in the order of the database records, retaining only those key-pointer pairs that have not been subtracted;
> sorting the file thus obtained;
> reconstructing the higher level index.

This simple approach is justified by the very short duration of the whole of this treatment—a few minutes on a small computer. In addition, each time the number of records in the database approaches 4900, we allow for an automatic indication to the operator that a restructuring operation is necessary, in order to delete those records logically subtracted.

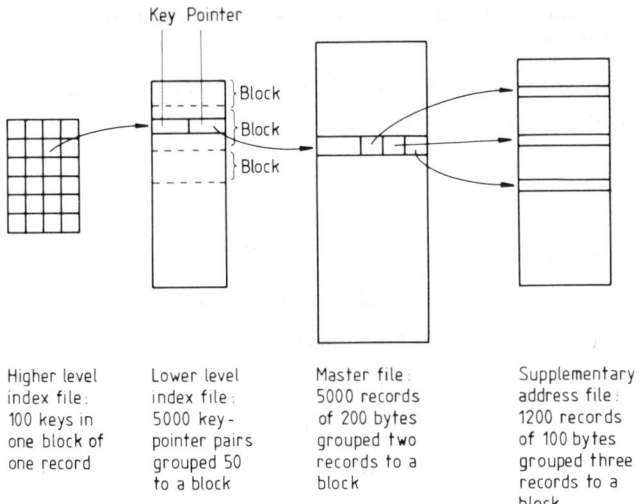

Key Pointer

}Block
}Block
}Block

| Higher level index file: 100 keys in one block of one record | Lower level index file: 5000 key-pointer pairs grouped 50 to a block | Master file: 5000 records of 200 bytes grouped two records to a block | Supplementary address file: 1200 records of 100 bytes grouped three records to a block |

Fig. 3.11

Comment: We can separate the higher level index file from the lower level index file, but we will not group the key-pointer pairs of the lower level index into tables constituting one record per block. We accept the slight loss of performance thus produced, in order to profit from the system-sort (a manufacturer's standard program) for the index file, instead of writing a special program.

The resulting structure therefore takes the form shown in Fig. 3.11 below.

### 3.3.9.4.2 Case 2

We decided in the preceding section to use an indexed structure with two index levels for case 2 as for case 1. In spite of the larger number of keys, we arrive at the same number of levels because of the greater allowable block size. But if (as in the preceding case) we used a lower level index containing one key-pointer record per record of the database, we would have to do a fairly substantial sort (50 000 records) at each addition/subtraction. Of course, such a sort lasts only a few minutes on a medium-sized computer, but there is no reason to waste this time. In this case the volume to be treated justifies the use of more complicated programming; we can therefore keep the following structure:

database file: one record per block (to reduce the volumes transferred during possible selections, which are more numerous), overflow area at the end of the file.

lower level index file: one record per block containing a table of 280 key-pointer pairs (of which we will use only 200 entries on creation, the rest being available for later additions); one overflow area of a few blocks at the end of the file.

higher level index file: one record of 50 000/200 = 250 keys, in a table;

supplementary address file: as for case 1.

Let us verify that the wastage of space in the index (due to the partially filled blocks) is acceptable:

80 (cost space) × 7 bytes × 250 blocks = 140 000 bytes.

The size of the lower level index is:

250 blocks × 280 × 7 = 490 000 bytes.

The size of the higher level index is:

250 × 4 = 1000 bytes.

The total size of the database and its indexes is therefore:

11 500 000 + 491 000 = 11 991 000 bytes.

The wastage in the index represents:

(140 000/11 991 000) × 100 = 1.16%

which is minimal even if we add the overflow area (of 20 blocks, for example) at the end of the file.

The + − operations can be carried out by marking in the database and in the index for subtraction, by writing at the end of the database file and in the overflow area of each block (even at the end of the index file) for addition.

Restructuring operations can be done by recopying those database records not subtracted into a new database file, at the same time building up a file of key-pointer pairs, and by sorting this file by key, then by recopying it into the tables—partial blocks—at the same time producing the higher level index.


### 3.3.4.9.3 Case 3

We can suppose that the study of the key-address transformation (allowing us to calculate the address of the record in the index where the database address is found) has been carried out. From this study, we can suppose that we have decided that the following index structure should be used to reduce the number of duplicates (Fig. 3.12).

Each block contains a single record. This is contained in a table of 280 key-pointer pairs (as in case 2). The 280th key-pointer pair is in fact a pointer to the general overflow area. On account of the considerable number of duplicates in certain cases, we must split each table of 280 key-pointer pairs into two unequal parts: an 'addressable' part of 50 key-pointer pairs (which can theoretically be accessed using hash coding); and a 'non-addressable' part of 230 key-pointer pairs reached from the addressable part when there are duplicates, and where the 230th points to the general overflow area, thus increasing the size of the non-addressable part.

Therefore the first duplicate record found on creation of the database (by a collision with a record already occupying one of the first 50 addresses in the table) is stored in the 51st address, the second in the 52nd, etc. Duplicate keys for the addressable part are therefore stored in the same block. Since certain keys have several duplicates, and since keys stored in the same block do not have any duplicates, a certain degree of compensation is produced. When a non-addressable part overflows, it overflows into a *complete* table of 280 key-pointer pairs,

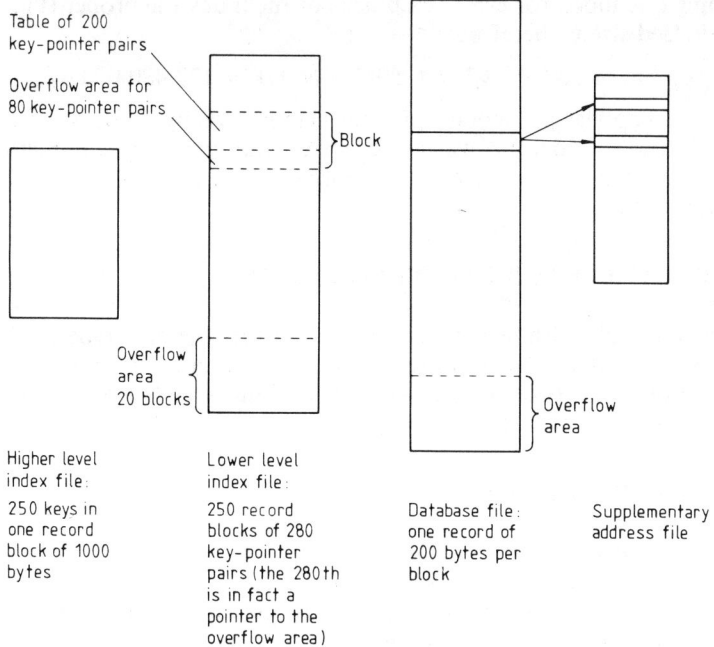

Table of 200
key-pointer pairs

Overflow area for
80 key-pointer pairs

Block

Overflow
area
20 blocks

Overflow
area

Higher level
index file:

250 keys in
one record
block of 1000
bytes

Lower level
index file:

250 record
blocks of 280
key-pointer
pairs (the 280th
is in fact a
pointer to the
overflow area)

Database file:
one record of
200 bytes per
block

Supplementary
address file

Fig. 3.12

placed in the general overflow area, and whose 280th element serves in turn as an overflow pointer, etc.

We must calculate the size of the index file to verify that it is acceptable. Let us suppose that the formula for the key-address transformation allows us in fact to access 4 million addresses (of which we know that at most 500 000 can contain keys). In addition, we must allow a size-increase factor of 280/50 on account of the non-addressable overflow areas in each block, and a general overflow area

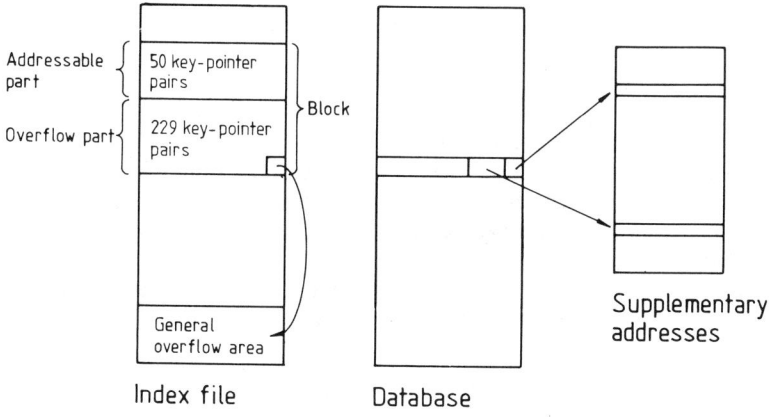

Addressable
part

50 key-pointer
pairs

Block

Overflow part

229 key-pointer
pairs

General
overflow area

Supplementary
addresses

Index file          Database

Fig. 3.13

containing one block for every ten blocks of the index file proper (Fig. 3.13). The desired size is therefore:

$$4 \times 10^6 \times 7 \times (280/50) \times 1.1 = 172\,480\,000 \text{ bytes}.$$

Since the database proper occupies only 115 million bytes, the solution given here leads to a considerable wastage of space. But by avoiding numerous disk accesses during selections, and costly reorganizations, we can save a valuable amount of time.

## 3.4 STRUCTURES FOR HISTORY DATABASES

This section deals with structures adapted to the 'history' type of database whose essential characteristics are: file creation, and addition of records by accumulation in the order of arrival; and fixed or variable length records, not modifiable nor removable.

### 3.4.1 Sample History Databases

#### 3.4.1.1 The 'Invoice History' File

This file holds the various pieces of information that appear on an invoice and are not stored elsewhere (such as the customer's name): invoice number, date, delivery details, total amount invoiced, taxes added, item numbers of the articles invoiced and their corresponding quantities, prices of these articles and the billing date, discounts, etc.
This information is used for:

fixed term commercial statistics;
marketing investigations and studies such as:
'How many items of category 17 did we sell during March in North America?'
'What is the sales total and the total tonnage of item number AC12-47 sold during the second half-year?'
'Retrieve and print all the invoices of customer number ...'

#### 3.4.1.2 The 'Stock History' File

This file holds the various pieces of information associated with the reception and dispatch of stock of various articles used by the company: item number, date and type of movement of stock (reception, dispatch, return to the supplier, order to the supplier), quantity, etc. This information is used for:
item usage statistics;
investigation of charging by cost-center, budget allocation analysis;
ventilation of deliveries by suppliers (date, quantity, price).

#### 3.4.1.3 The Ledger

This file holds all the bookkeeping transactions for a year, allowing investigations and audits difficult to obtain by other methods: the total and the details of the debits and credits on a particular account coming from a specified source in a given month, for example.

The case of an 'invoice' history illustrates a structure with a variable length record (the invoice). The other two examples make do with fixed-length records.

### 3.4.2 Fundamental Operations on History Databases

*Addition*: This is performed on an entire record of fixed or variable length. Each new record is written immediately after the preceding records; the index tables, if any, are updated.

*Restructuring*: This involves the deletion of 'expired' records; if necessary, reorganizes (sorts) the database according to a simple criterion—for example, by date, if that helps the selections (see section 3.4.4 for more details).

*Selection*: This involves picking out the records that respect certain criteria, among which the date plays a privileged role. These records are listed, recopied onto an 'extract' file or only used for calculating the totals of certain of their fields.

The *modification* and *subtraction* operations are in principle forbidden, since they are meaningless. In fact, one can see that it is useful to be able to access certain fields in order to modify their contents, but this procedure only helps to correct errors. It is then often difficult to specify a record to be modified when it has been retrieved by selection. For example, two accounting transactions identical with respect to date, amount, account number, and only differing in their wording, are for this reason difficult to distinguish and therefore to specify. In addition to the 'normal' selection criteria, we have to make use of the idea of *order*: to modify the first, the second, the $N$th record that satisfies these criteria.

The nature of these operations implies that the structure of history files will be studied only with respect to two major criteria:

the logical structure of the records and their length (fixed or variable);
the selections to be planned for.

The addition operation is limited to a write operation at the end of the file; the restructuring operation is limited to a selective recopy of the file, together with a sort as appropriate—this does not need an elaborate structure.

### 3.4.3 Database Levels—Hierarchies

This section deals with the structure of a database with respect of the logical structure of the data it contains. This structure sometimes appears as a hierarchy, as the following example shows.

Let us consider a 'customer' database where each record contains the customer number, name, address; knowing the customer number (assumed to be the key), we can find right away, in a record, the rest of the information about the customer—we will say that the database *has a single level*. Let us suppose now that we associate with each customer the list of invoices that concern him.

For each invoice we will store the invoice number, its date, its amount. The quantity of invoices associated with each customer is 0, 1, 2, ..., or $N$. If $N$ is not limited in advance, it is not possible to know beforehand the length of the logical record required for storing the invoices of a given customer; we can say that the customer file *has two levels*. The first level is that of the record—number–name–address—the second that of the invoices. The structure of such a database is, for example, as shown in Fig. 3.14. Let us suppose now that with each invoice we associate the payments (financial transactions) that concern it. For each invoice we have to store a certain number of financial transactions, each of which has a date, a transaction type and an amount. If the number of transactions per invoice is not limited in advance, we need a third level in the preceding database to take account of the payments.

The example above illustrates the idea of *levels of* logical records. A logical record with $N$ levels is stored in a logical record spanning in general $N$ physical files. The number of physical files in fact depends on the sizes of the physical records required for storing the successive parts of level, 1, 2, ... $N$; if two parts have the same physical length, they can, if desired, share the same file. This concept of level is more often required for history databases than for master file databases—that is why we introduce it here. The corresponding physical structure must provide a means of access to all records of level $X$ corresponding to a given record of level $X$-1; knowing of a given invoice (we have already read its record), we must be able to find the corresponding payments records directly. This may be done in two ways:

1. By interconnecting the various records of level $X$ by means of pointers, and by connecting the first one to the record of level $X$-1, as in the above figure. In this way we build up a collection of records called a 'list' or a 'chain', because the various records (or 'links') are connected by means of pointers.
2. By connecting the record of level $X$-1 to a small index (sometimes called 'a

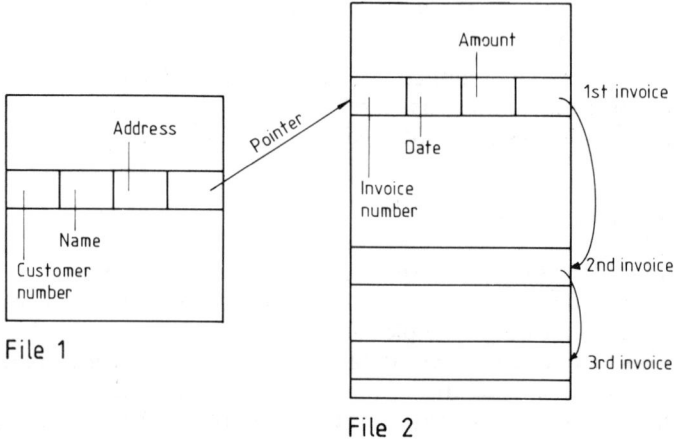

Fig. 3.14

70

pointer array') giving the list of key-pointer pairs that allows access to all records of level $X$. This latter method, more complicated to implement from a programming point of view, allows more rapid access (since it is more direct) to the records of level $X$.

Whatever the structure choosen, the restructuring of a file at various levels groups successive records of level $X$ together, when they depend on the same record of level $X$-1. From a terminology point of view, note that the record of level $X$ is often called the 'son' or 'successor' and the record of level $X$-1 is called the 'father' or 'predecessor'.

### 3.4.4 Structures, Lists and Selection Indexes

This section deals with the structures of history databases with respect to the selections planned. A history database is filled by successive additions that write the records to be stored, one after another. It is useful from time to time to do a restructuring operation that:

deletes records that are too old;
sorts the lowest level records by date;
regroups into successive records the sons of the same father;
reconstructs an index by date that contains, for each date, only the first record at the lowest level corresponding to that date.

The privileged part played by the date in the case of history databases can be explained by the following observation: those users who make selections always impose a date constraint ('after 31 March', 'between 31 March and 30 June'). Since history databases are generally massive, it is necessary to speed up selections by reducing the part of the database where the search is being done. Since, on the other hand, the data index is small (generally as many or fewer date-pointer pairs as working days in 12 months), we often store it in the header of the lowest level history file.

Therefore from now on we assume that every history database is supplied with its data index, and we no longer refer to that aspect of its structure after the following observation.

Most often, an item of history data is concerned with a year or a fraction of a year (month, quarter, half-year). When this period of time is over it is not in our interest to destroy the file, nor even to remove it completely from disk once we have made an archive copy of it. For an annual file, for example, it is better to consider the file as *cyclic* and to make it cover, for example, the last 12 (or 13) months, than to consider it as *periodic* (which makes it cover the year). Thus, at the end of February 1976, we for instance, destroy everything before March 1975, to keep a real 12-month historical record. Often, even, we only destroy information before 1 February 1975, to preserve 13 months; this allows us to 'compare a given period to the corresponding one a year ago', something very useful to managers. Apart from the date index, a history database is structured along the same lines as a master file database; according to the selection types required, we can build up indexes on any given field, existence tables, lists connecting (by pointers) records fulfilling the same condition. These indexes, tables

71

and lists can point to any file level. We do not therefore indicate a specific structure for history files, but only note that:

1. The maintenance of index files is always done during restructuring operations. Therefore an index file always has two parts: one unsorted corresponding to the part added since the previous restructuring operation, and one sorted corresponding to data added before the restructuring.
2. The addition of a record requires the creation of pointers that point to it in each of the *previous* records of the various lists (chains of records connected by pointers) that are spread over the file. Nevertheless, it is extremely expensive to run through a list, record by record, following the pointers in order to find the last record. Since lists in history databases are generally long, we allow for a *table of extremities* in the file header. This table contains for each list the addresses of the beginning and end of the list. Direct access to the end of the list will allow a rapid update of the pointer. Access to the beginning of the list helps to speed up the selections of records belonging to that list.
3. A list structure is a bit dangerous to use; if, for example, a list is broken due to a software or hardware failure, it is sometimes difficult to spot this and to put it right. It is therefore necessary to avoid using too many and too long lists. Furthermore, it is wise to produce some 'integrity programs' which ensure that no lists are broken and which repair them if they are.

## 3.5 STRUCTURES FOR OPEN ITEM DATABASES

This section deals with structures adapted to the 'open item' type of database whose essential characteristics are:

logical data structure made of records including a 'header' part (fixed length), and 'details' (whose quantity is undefined) each of which is fixed length;

many additions/subtractions of details to/from a given header, many additions/subtractions of entire records (header plus details).

the possibility of headers existing without details, but not of details existing without headers.

### 3.5.1 Sample Open Item Database

Let us consider a manufacturer's 'order' file organized by ordered item. Each record consists of a header (containing an item number, its name and various characteristics) and as many details as there are orders to be supplied for that item. Each detail contains an order number, a delivery date and the quantity ordered. After a promotional sales campaign for certain items, the database grows considerably, and many details are added to the items concerned. When the dispatching has been done, the file size decreases proportionally, and the details corresponding to the orders supplied are erased. The structure consists of two physical files for the data (a 'headers' file and a 'details' file) and various index files (including one for the headers); it will be identical in nature to that used for the history database with two levels (section 3.4.3).

### 3.5.2 Fundamental Operations and Appropriate Structure

*Addition*: This is performed by adding the header (if it does not already exist) and the details chained to the header or to the last existing detail.

*Subtraction*: This usually consists of the deletion of the details, one by one or in small groups. When a header no longer has details associated with it, we often also delete it. We re-establish the pointers 'over' a deleted detail, by making its predecessor point to its successor.

*Modification*: This applies usually to a detail, where one of its fields is changed. It could happen that this operation is not provided for, and that it is good enough simply to delete and then to recreate the detail in question.

*Restructuring*: the essential aim here is to recover the space left by many deletions. It is done by recopying: successive headers that are to be left are recopied in the new header file. For each header, all the details are recopied in the appropriate order within the chain, regrouping them, and thus a new details file is created.

*Selection and relevant structures*: here are two privileged types of selection, the type that allows the retrieval of the headers and the type that allows the retrieval of the 'detail keys'. The detail key is the contents of the field of this detail that allows the detail to be distinguished from the other details of the same header chain, as, for instance the order number in the above example. The rapid search of headers is done with the help of a classical index, or hash code.

Concerning the details keys, we can:

1. Build a table of extremities (if the number of these keys is small) or an index file (if the number is large), and connect by pointers the details corresponding to the same key. The index file, if any, must (as a table of extremities) contain the addresses of the two extremities of the chain of the same key built in this way, with the address of the end of the chain being used for additions, as in note 2 of section 3.4.4.
2. Build an existence table indicating for each header record whether or not it contains the key in question. This method is only feasible when the number of possible keys is small.

Apart from the two privileged selection types above, selections on other details fields or header fields are done using specific index files.

The following comments apply to open item databases:

1. When the presence of an index allows direct access to a member of a details chain, it is impossible to retrieve another detail or the chain if one of the following three pointer systems has not been adopted:

   (a) connect the last detail of the chain to the header, thus producing a 'cyclic' chain (or 'ring' or 'closed chain'),
   (b) connect each detail to its predecessor at the same time as to its successor,
   (c) maintain in each detail a pointer towards its header.

2. The fairly high instability that characterizes open item databases, because of the large number of updates, increases even more the danger associated with the use of pointers (see note 3, section 3.4.4). The presence of *intersecting* chains, like the details chain of the same item header and the details chain of the same order (see the example in section 3.5.1 above), makes the integrity of an open item database particularly 'fragile'.

Whenever possible, we therefore avoid planning for updates of such structures in real time, or in a terminal environment. It is also vital to study with great care the procedures and programs that allow the restoration or the verification of the integrity of the database.

3. A second consequence of the instability and of the resulting need for frequent restructuring operations is the very high cost of updating or reconstructing any indexes and existence tables.
4. As a general rule, an open item database is more powerful and more general than a structure of the master file or history type.

With the exception of history files with more than two levels, these structures may be considered as particular cases of the open item structures. But we must avoid using an open item structure when there is no need for one, as it is more costly to program and to use (processing time, disk accesses) and more dangerous with respect to the integrity of the chains of pointers. As a general rule, the use of such a structure involves a considerably large number of disk accesses, degrading for this reason the performance of the computer; this degradation is clearly less noticeable on computers running in a multiprogramming environment, especially if they have several independent disk channels.

## 3.6 COMPLEX STRUCTURES—OPEN CONTENT DATABASES

### 3.6.1 Evolution of a Database

The structures that we have introduced up to this point are fairly easy to understand and indeed to implement. They are standard and they do not baffle the analyst by their novelty. They have, however, a major inconvenience: they are not well adapted to the *evolution* of the database. A database generally evolves in one or several of the following ways:

the size of a given field may vary, going from four to six digits, for example;
the number of fields may change—we may from a given point in time want to handle new pieces of information and 'forget' old ones;
more rarely, we may want to connect existing data to other data; for example: if a 'customer' database contains a customer's address, and an 'outstanding payments' database contains the list of bills to be paid by each customer, we may wish to act *quickly* to select customers in a certain region whose outstanding invoiced total exceeds a certain amount.

In order to do the latter we can, of course, make separate selections on these databases, each with its own criterion (region or amount respectively), then sort these selections by customer number and keep only the records that have the same customer number. But this process would be slow and quite complicated.

To obtain a result, and be able to do it frequently, the two databases in question must be connected by pointers to the customer number. The resulting database will then have a structure of the open item type, whose headers will be the customers and whose details will be each customer's invoices. The addition of this new system of pointers, connecting existing data to other data, is an *evolution* of the database, in the same way as the addition of new fields; it is an evolution in the *relationships between data.*

Comment: The evolution of a database in one of the above ways is in general much less frequent than the updates of the database; we can observe, for example, that a database that is subject to + − and MOD operations on a daily basis remains for 2 months without evolving. The aim of this section is to describe some structures and processing methods that provide a certain flexibility for the evolution of a database. Nevertheless we must keep in mind the idea of *cost* of evolution: the evolution requires human effort and computer processing; the ability to evolve (called the 'flexibility' or 'openness' of the database) imposes a more complex structure, less efficient processing of + −, MOD, SEL, an increased storage cost and a more difficult—and therefore more demanding—programming load. We therefore have to find a compromise between the cost of the *flexibility* (used only during evolution stages) and the performance during the frequent repetitive operations, between the programming costs and the maintenance costs.

### 3.6.2 Addition of New Fields to a Database

Of the three types of database evolution, the most frequent is the addition of fields. After the installation of a database we often notice that certain details have been forgotten, or that some data exist that we would like to handle at the same time as certain data already present in the database. The aim of this section is to review the methods that can be used and their corresponding structures.

#### *3.6.2.1 Addition in an Existing Record*

The first method that comes to mind consists of:

determining the physical file to which we want to add a new field;
redefining the record description for this file by including the new field;
recompiling all the programs that access this file with the new record description;
if the file has increased in size (because of the lack of free space in the record), copying the old file to a new file with the desired record size;
filling in the new field by means of MOD operations on this new file;
testing the various recompiled programs with suitable data;
keeping a 'backup' copy of the previous version of the database and programs;
for a short time, and if it is possible, maintaining the two versions of the database concurrently and comparing the results.

This process is easy to formulate. The implementation, however, requires care and accurate planning if we want to respect the integrity of the data and not to forget recompilations, testing, etc. The best way of going about this is to record *at the time of the initial creation of the database and its programs*:

the descriptions of the files and routines stored in libraries;
the programs to be recompiled and the order of their recompilation;
the tests to be done, with their corresponding data.

We shall see by the end of this book that good design of the programs for database creation/maintenance considerably reduces the total number of programs that access the database. Apart from the significant saving of writing and of maintenance of programs associated with the use of a database, the number of recompilations and tests is reduced and can easily be organized and planned methodically; the evolution of a database is thus easier than we would have thought.

We can see that the above method, involving the modification of record descriptions, applies equally to the *subtraction* and the *size modification* of fields. Generally speaking, this method is valid as long as the evolution of a database does not take place more than a few times a year—which is common in business problem situations. It is not automatic, but requires the intervention of programmers; and it ensures that the structure of the files stays compatible with the good performance of the programs (see Chapter 4, section 4.1.5.: the 'window' principle).

### 3.6.2.2 Using Parallel Files

When it is not possible to add the new field(s) to the record existing in file A, a make-shift solution is to create a new file B intended for the additions. This file B contains one record for each record of file A that it completes, and in the same relative position; record number *N* of A is completed by record number *N* of B. File B is said to be 'parallel' to A. This method does not use pointers and does not alter A, but it prevents A being sorted (because B would not be sorted) and does not remove the necessity to alter the programs, nor to carry out the entire procedure as described in section 3.6.2.1 above.

The use of this parallel file method is worthwhile when one field (or more) to be inserted in the file must frequently be used as selection criterion. In this case, and if the records of the parallel file are small, the file becomes a low level index for the main database, generally unsorted.

### 3.6.2.3 Using Supplementary Files and Pointers: Total Opening

### 3.6.2.3.1 Single Addition
We have often to add fields *only to some* of the records of the database. For example, if only 20% of the records must accept a group of additional fields, it does not make sense to plan for the addition of a group of fields to *every* record of the database, whether by incorporating it in each record or by using a parallel file; this would waste a great deal of space. Consequently, we build a 'file of supplementary fields' and make the appropriate records of the main file point to the corresponding records of the supplementary file.

*Example 3.12* Let us consider a 'customer' database where 20% of the

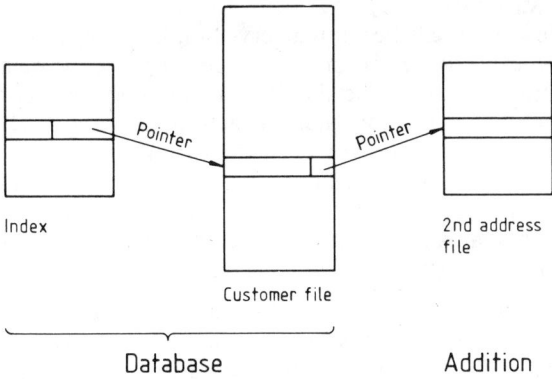

Index                Customer file         2nd address file

Database           Addition

Fig. 3.15

customers have a mailing address different from their billing address. The structure is as shown in Fig. 3.15.

### 3.6.2.3.2 Double Addition

The 'supplementary file plus pointer' method can be used for *different* fields (or groups of fields). Thus in the previous example, if we wish to add a new 'banking address' data item, we can to store it in the 'second address' file and point to it from the main database. The auxiliary second address' will then contain *two* groups of different fields.

     We must take the following precautions:

1.    Minimize the space wastage due to the storage of logical groups of fields of *different* physical sizes. This could be done, for example, by declaring one (very large) record per block, and by dividing it into fairly small 'sub-records' (one word, one byte, or even a half-byte for example) that we could organize ourselves. Each field (or group of fields) will thus be stored in a certain number of consecutive subrecords. The database management software can write and read the fields (or groups of fields) directly to or from the subrecords.

2.    Take precautions against any possible breakage of ('return') pointers pointing back to the main database and/or of 'field group type' codes, by allowing for the production of a suitable cleanup program and procedure capable of reconstructing and organizing the auxiliary file according to the order of the main database.

### 3.6.2.3.3 Repeated Additions: Opening the Database

There is nothing, in principle, to prevent us from extending the previous method to as many fields or groups of fields as we wish. Each data type must be identified by a code type and pointed to by the main database, which becomes 'open' or 'extensible'. In fact, if we wish to have an 'unlimited' openness, we must take certain precautions:

1.    Since the number of additional pointers to be stored in the main database could increase indefinitely, we must allow for a *pointer structure*, or

'linkage structure'.

2. Since the structure is becoming very complex in terms of the number of fields that can exist in a record, it is necessary to implement software that allows information in the database to be read, written and retrieved without requiring a recompilation each time the database evolves.
3. Each time the database evolves (if the various structural, software, and procedural transformations are not automatic) we need to ensure that the new database is still 'downwards' compatible with the old one; the existing programs must not be affected by this evolution except in an automatic, transparent and reliable way.

A few examples allow us to present all these ideas in detail. However, we can already see in plain terms the software characteristics of open databases: complexity, relative inefficiency (number of disk accesses and extra storage space required for the pointers). Remember therefore that the openness or flexibility of a database is costly: we must ensure that this flexibility is really necessary *before* committing ourselves to the construction and use of an open database.

### 3.6.3 Open Content Databases

There are several ways of constructing open content databases. We present here only a single method which is relatively easy to understand and to put into operation. As it stands, the difficulty in programming the method is nevertheless immeasurable compared with the preceding structures. The programming cost, however, is justified by the total opening of the database, as well as by its 'integral' nature. Indeed, it is possible, with the structure presented, to integrate all the data for a medium-sized company, representing roughly a thousand different pieces of information (fields).

#### 3.6.3.1 Definitions

Since a database must contain numerous fields, the first necessity is to define these fields and group them logically; this step is known as 'construction of the data dictionary', a definition used by:

1. the analyst who designs the database;
2. the database administrator who keeps it up to date;
3. the database user who extracts information from it;
4. the programs that access the database.

Point 1 above requires that this definition be represented in a graphical form suitable for the analysis. Points 2 and 3 require a representation of the 'cross-referenced list' type. Point 4 requires that the definition be represented in the form of a data description table, stored in a file.

Finally, since the representation of data into groups other than the logical records is done using chains of pointers and secondary indexes, we can build up a *table of chains and indexes*. This table will be used as much by the database administrator as by the update programs, which, at each update of a logical

**Table 3.6**

| Notation | Significance |
|---|---|
| GF | Group of fields (divided into fields) |
| F | Field (not subdivided) |
| D→ | Detail of a chain of detail fields linked by pointers: |
| | F→ F→ F→ etc. · · · A 'D→' is 'a field plus a pointer'. |
| DG→ | Detail of a chain of groups of fields. |
| | Each DG is subdivided into elementary fields. |
| | Each group is linked to the following by a pointer: |
| | GF→ GF→ GF→ etc. · · · |
| | We frequently meet DG→ and rarely D→. In any case, the presence of a link by pointers indicated by the arrow → involves also that of an *implicit* pointer field P, not represented in the structure and serving to link all the D→ or DG→ to each other. |
| P | Pointer: field serving as a pointer |

record, complete the necessary chains and indexes ( see section 3.6.3.4).

The analyst's view is called the 'conceptual view'; the database user and his programs' view is called the 'external view'; the actual data file and pointer structure is called the 'internal view' of the database.

*3.6.3.1.1 Graphical Representation of a Data Structure*
(Table 3.6) shows some similarity to the FD description of the COBOL language. It involves *one* logical record.

*Example 3.13  Record of a Master File.*  Fig. 3.16 shows:
the group of fields $GF_1$ (associated with the group name 'CUSTOMER'),
the horizontal and vertical lines giving the subdivision of $GF_1$,
the    fields    $F_2$ (associated with NUMBER);
                         $F_3$ (associated with NAME);
                         $F_4$ (associated with ADDRESS);
                         $F_5$ (associated with AGENT-CODE).

We usually do the following:

align the fields of the same 'COBOL level' along the same vertical subdivision line, these fields being subdivisions of the same field group;
number each field or group of fields;
write the significance of this field or group, either at its side, or in a nomen-

| Representation | | Analogy in COBOL | | |
|---|---|---|---|---|
| $GF_1$ | 01 | CUSTOMER | | |
| ├─$F_2$ | | 02  NUMBER | PIC | 9(8) |
| ├─$F_3$ | | 02  NAME | PIC | X(30) |
| ├─$F_4$ | | 02  ADDRESS | PIC | X(80) |
| └─$F_5$ | | 02  AGENT-CODE | PIC | 99 |

Fig. 3.16   Record of a master file.

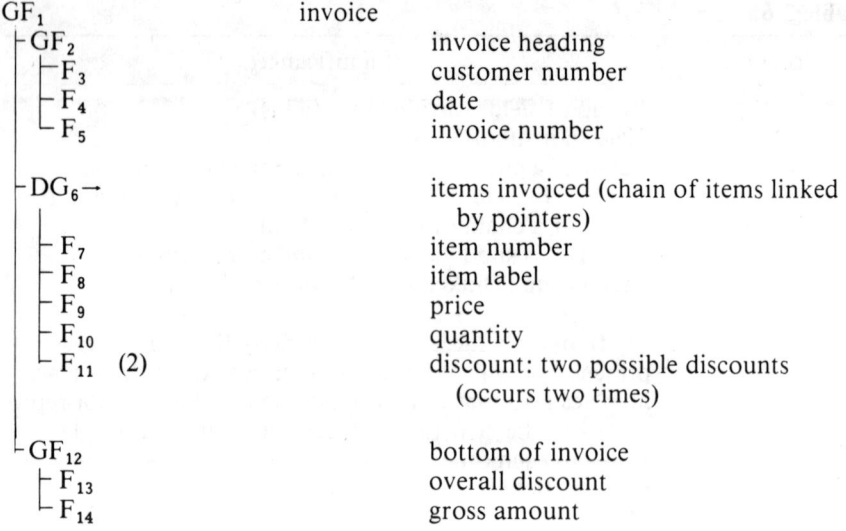

| $GF_1$ | | invoice |
|---|---|---|
| $GF_2$ | | invoice heading |
| $F_3$ | | customer number |
| $F_4$ | | date |
| $F_5$ | | invoice number |
| $DG_6 \rightarrow$ | | items invoiced (chain of items linked by pointers) |
| $F_7$ | | item number |
| $F_8$ | | item label |
| $F_9$ | | price |
| $F_{10}$ | | quantity |
| $F_{11}$ | (2) | discount: two possible discounts (occurs two times) |
| $GF_{12}$ | | bottom of invoice |
| $F_{13}$ | | overall discount |
| $F_{14}$ | | gross amount |

Fig. 3.17   Record of a 'two-level invoice history' file.

    clature table opposite the number of the field or group;
follow each field or group by a number in brackets if this field or group is repeated several times (OCCURS of COBOL, DIMENSION of FORTRAN).

*Example 3.14   Record of a Two-Level Invoice History File.*   In Fig. 3.17, 'level 1' represents $GF_2$ and $GF_{12}$; 'level 2' represents $DG_6 \rightarrow$, which would normally be stored in a separate file; we see that we must not confuse 'COBOL level' and 'logical database level'. Fig. 3.18 shows the record of an 'orders outstanding' file.

### 3.6.3.1.2 Data Dictionary
The purpose of the data dictionary is to:

    complete the graphical representation,
provide for each GF, F, D→, DG→ or P:
    its symbolic number,
    the explanation of its contents, its creation conditions,
        validity date, access permission, etc.,
    its 'level' (equivalent to the COBOL level and to the
        indentation towards the right in the graphical representation) and the 'father' field (number of the GF to which this data should be attached),
    the length (size) expressed in words, bytes, half-bytes or
        bits,
    its capacity (maximum length expressed in number of
        characters if the data is alphanumeric, or possible sign and number of digits if the data is numeric: if the data is packed decimal, it is necessary to supply the minimum and maximum values (in the algebraic sense

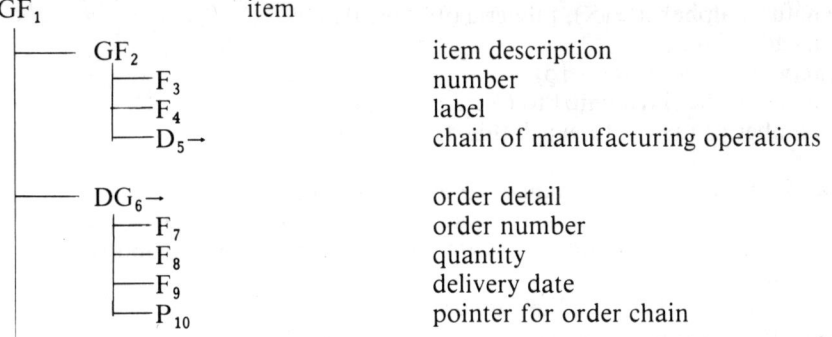

| | |
|---|---|
| GF₁ | item |
| GF₂ | item description |
| F₃ | number |
| F₄ | label |
| D₅→ | chain of manufacturing operations |
| DG₆→ | order detail |
| F₇ | order number |
| F₈ | quantity |
| F₉ | delivery date |
| P₁₀ | pointer for order chain |

Each order consists of a chain linking its different details. The order number, which is redundant, serves to reconstruct the chain as required, and to produce certain lists. This structure is completed by:

one index per item pointing to $GF_1$

one index per order pointing to the first detail for this order (head of the chain)

$F_{11}$ (12)   total quantity on order for each of the 12 months of the year (redundant)

Fig. 3.18   Record of an 'orders outstanding' file.

and the step size), the information for possible packing/unpacking (names of the subroutines required, etc.),
the file pointed to (in the case of P), the symbolic name(s)
for this data used in the programs,
its validity code, used when the field is deleted, while
waiting for it to be physically removed from the files and the dictionary
by a restructuring operation on the database.

The dictionary also contains:

one list by data number;
one alphabetical list by symbolic name;
one list of the files and programs using each piece of data;
one list of the data chains and indexes allowing individual rapid accesses. For each chain, there is a list of update subroutines or procedures.

The data dictionary is presented in the form of a listing, created by appropriate software forming part of the 'data description language'.

### 3.6.3.1.3 Data Description Table
This table is a representation (stored in a file) of a data structure. It is intended to direct the programs which access the database, and contains one record per data item. The records are stored in the order of the data numbers and contain:

the data number;
the type GF, F, D→, DG→ or P;
the level: 0 highest, 1 lower, etc.;

the nature: alphabetic (X), numeric (9), bit (01);

the length or size;

the repetition factor (or zero);

the name of the file pointed to (for a pointer);

the number of the GF to which this data is attached;

the validity code;

if the data are packed, the names of the subroutines for
   packing and unpacking, and the access parameters for these subroutines
   required to read (decode) or write (encode) the data in the appropriate
   format;

the name of the file where the data are stored;

a code indicating whether or not the data are described in the
   linkage file (if it is not, the GF or DG→ which contains it is).

This table is recreated at each evolution of the database. It is read and kept in memory by the programs that access the database and use it to interpret the contents of files. *The modification of the table replaces the recompilation of these programs during an evolution.*

This table is created and updated by the database administrator, who expresses the structure evolutions in a 'data description language'.

### 3.6.3.1.4 *Table of Chains and Indexes; Lists and Rings*

These data structures used in creating an open content database are not generally adapted to all the uses of this type of database. For example, the 'two-level invoice history' structure defined in example 3.14 above is not suitable for rapid searching for all the invoices of a given customer; we can, however, adapt the structure for this type of search:

by adding a pointer $P_{15}$ to the field $GF_1$;

by linking to each other all the invoices for a given customer
   with the help of these pointers; each invoice will then point to the
   following one (Fig. 3.19);

by building up a secondary index, whose key is the customer
   number, and which contains one record for each customer, with:

   customer number,
   the address of the linkage chain for the first invoice of this
      customer,
   the address of the linkage chain for the last invoice of this
      customer (see section 3.6.3.2 on linkage chain).

Of course we can also do without pointer $P_{15}$, and put in the secondary index one record per invoice containing:

the customer number;

the invoice number;

the address of the linkage chain for this invoice.

The above example shows the need, for databases containing a large number of different pieces of information, to link the pieces of information to each other using chains and/or suitable indexes. If we create these chains and

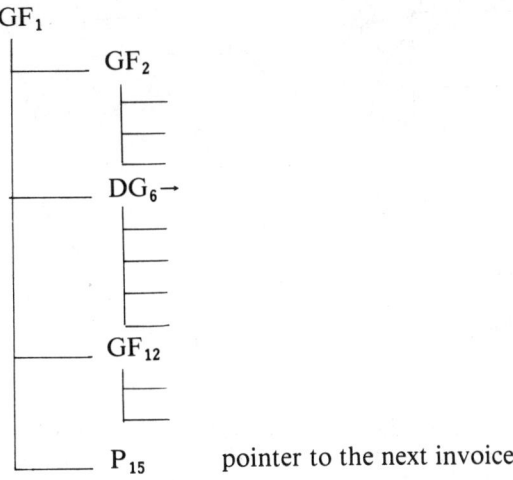

GF$_1$

GF$_2$

DG$_6 \rightarrow$

GF$_{12}$

P$_{15}$      pointer to the next invoice

Fig. 3.19

indexes, we must update them when the database itself is updated (addition of invoices, for example) or when the database evolves. In order to make these updates automatic, we create a descriptive table for the chains and indexes, used by those programs which update the database or are involved in the evolution of the database. At the same time, this table contains text describing the chains or indexes, used by the data administrator and for the documentation of the system. For each chain or index, the table contains, for example:

the number of the chain or index (identification), a descriptive
     text;
the type (chain or index);
the number of the field defining the chain or index (in the
     preceding example it would be F$_3$, the field number-of-customer);
the number of the pointer field, in the case of a chain (P$_{15}$ in the
     preceding example);
the name of the index file and the address of the first record
     available for additions, in the case of an index;
the name of the program or procedure to be executed in order
     to build up, reconstruct or update the chain or index.

We see that a logical chain in fact contains a certain number of physical chains, one for each value of the chainage criterion (same customer number, for example). Accessing any element of a chain must allow us to find *all* the elements. We achieve this by building up a *closed chain* or *ring* (Fig. 3.20); the 'last' element points to the first. When going through the chain, we only need to memorize the starting point so that, once we have returned to the same point we stop, as the end of the chain has been reached.

83

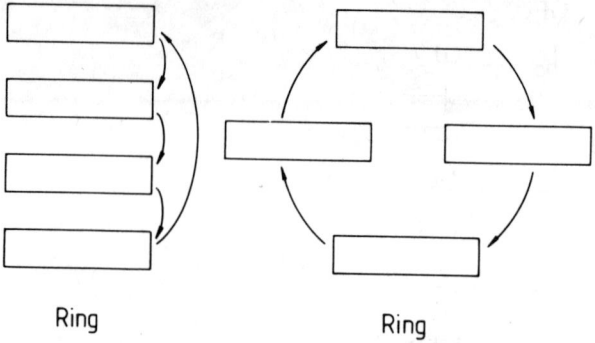

Ring                              Ring

Fig. 3.20   Rings.

The descriptive table for the chains and indexes contains, for each chain, the information allowing access to a 'head-of-chain file'. This file contains one record per existing chain, with the value of the definition field and the address of the 'first' (or even the 'last') element of the chain—this is the secondary index in the preceding example.

Thus, when we start anywhere other than at the beginning of a chain, we can read the value of the chainage criterion in this record. By then going to the head-of-chain file for the chain being considered, we find the addresses of the start and end of this chain. We can thus go through the chain starting from the beginning, or add an element to the end, if the order is important. The concepts of 'start', 'end' or 'ring' are not therefore essential; we choose the most suitable structure in each case. Likewise, we can replace the head-of-chain file by a second system of pointers, in the opposite sense to the preceding one, to go through the chain in reverse; we then talk of 'forward' and 'backward' pointers. The advantage of the file is essentially in building up a table of existing chains, or even to indicate the logical beginning; if this advantage is worthless, we do not use this file.

### 3.6.3.2 Linkage Structure

In an open content database, a large number of fields (elementary or group) is used. What is more, we reserve the right to add new fields frequently, to remove old fields and to add new links using pointers to data of the same or a different database. Finally, the logical records do not have fixed contents because:
they can contain chains of details DG→ or D→; *In a given record, certains fields may be missing.* For example, if a customer can have up to three addresses, but the second and third addresses exist only for certain customers, we will store only the existing addresses to save space.

The representation of data (graphical, in a dictionary or in a table) does not therefore guarantee the presence of a given field or record. We therefore use a *note* to indicate the actual presence of information in a given record.

In addition, the physical presence of a piece of information does not guarantee its validity; it may have been logically removed, or access to it may be reserved for certain persons (secret) or circumstances. The preceding note is

84

therefore accompanied by a *validity code*. We note the presence and accessibility of information in the 'linkage chain' of the record (so called because we can 'link' new notes on demand (to represent new fields) using pointers). A linkage chain, representing a given logical record, is built up of data descriptor links, each of which contains:

the field number (or name) (the same as in the dictionary or table);
the start address (or 'left-most address' or 'displacement') of the data in the file where it is stored;
the validity code for the data:
0 = deleted
1 = accessible without restriction
2, 3, ... = reserved access;
a pointer, used only for data of type DG→ (very frequent) that associates with each piece of data the one which logically follows it, by pointing to the address of its descriptive link;
a second pointer, used only for data of type GF and DG→, indicating the address (in the linkage chain) of the start of the description of the group of fields under consideration (that is, the address of the first link describing a component of the given GF or DG→);
a third pointer (optional) used for possible extensions of the chain (+ F) 'connected' to this link.

The data can be of type GF, F, D→, DG→, or P. The space they occupy in the file starts at the left-most address indicated, the length being given in the dictionary or table.

Note: If the type if GF, and if it contains only isolated F's, *all* the fields of this group are stored in the database file, without exception. The validity code then applies to the whole group. The possibility of representing a group instead of each field guarantees a certain degree of conciseness in the linkage chain. Without this conciseness, the linkage chain could well be as large as the record it represents. In practice, the use of groups reduces the size of the chain to less than 20% of that of the record, generally speaking.

If the type is D→, a certain number of identical fields are stored. Each one is followed by a pointer, whose existence is implied by the type itself, and which indicates the position of the following field. This pointer does not appear in the graphical representation other than by the arrow → which follows the D. The left-most address, indicated by the connection link, is that of the first detail field. If details of the same type logically follow the first in the database file, they will not be noted in the linkage file. The implicit pointer of each D→ is stored physically after the D→ to which it belongs, in the file where the data itself is stored.

If the type is DG→, there are two possibilities:

1. If the subdivisions of DG→ do not appear in the linkage file (because we have chosen *always* to store all the fields comprising this DG→ in the data base) the pointer implied by the arrow on the DG must be stored in the database itself because only the first DG→ in the chain will be stored in the linkage file. The DG→ is then processed—in fact—as a D→.
2. If the subdivisions of a DG→ do appear in the linkage file, the pointers

will also be there (see the example of an open content database at the end of this section).

### 3.6.3.2.1 Interconnections Among the Links
For reasons of efficiency, we usually group together the links in groups of 3 to 10. To each group we add a pointer, which indicates the next group and is used if necessary. An unused link is set to 0. We sometimes also add a pointer to the preceding group; this allows us to go through the linkage chain in reverse order to find certain pieces of information when we access the chain other than at its beginning (see multiple indexes, section 3.6.3.3).

A group and its pointer make up a logical record (or even a physical one) of the linkage file (Fig. 3.21).

### 3.6.3.2.2 Grouping of Links
A certain number of links (about 100, for example) comprise a physical record that fills an entire block. On construction of the linkage file, we take care to allow for *an overflow area* in each block. We will write here the groups of links comprising the logical remainder of the chains for the same block. This technique allows the number of disk accesses to be reduced at the cost of a slight wastage of space. The size of the overflow area depends on the *stability* of the database. The word stability means either 'update-stability' or 'evolution-stability':

addition/subtraction of data of the 'existing' type (as in non-open content databases), performed using the DML (data manipulation language): update;
the addition of new data types, performed using the DDL (data description language), followed by an assignment of their effective values: evolution.

Relatively stable databases make do with overflow areas covering some 20% of the size of the linkage; but in general a value of 30% to 50% is necessary if we wish to avoid frequent and costly reorganizations. Of course, the existence of an overflow area in each block does not allow us to dispense with the creation of a supplementary general area at *3.6.3.3 Storage Structure, FIFO and LIFO lists.*

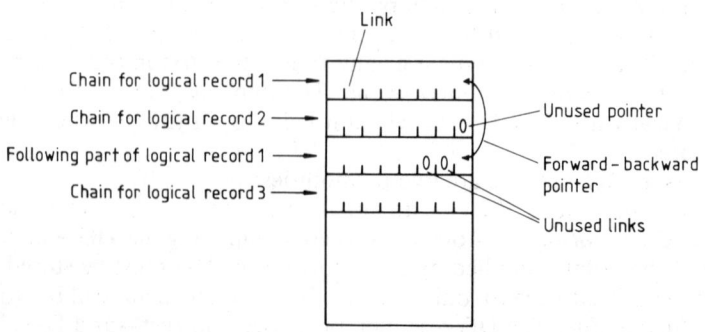

Fig. 3.21   Linkage file.

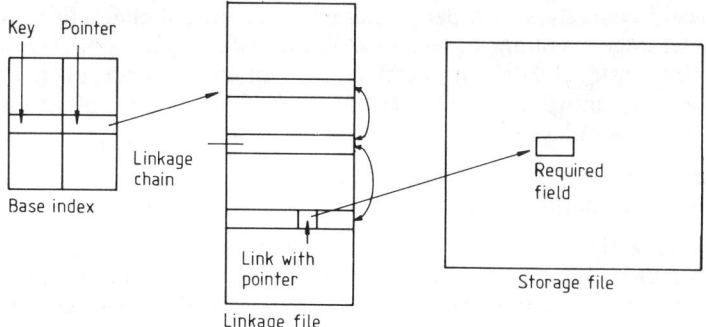

Key    Pointer

Linkage
chain

Base index

Link with
pointer

Linkage file

Required
field

Storage file

Fig. 3.22

### 3.6.3.3  Storage Structure, FIFO and LIFO Lists

This section describes the manner in which data is stored in the database. As a result of the graphical representation mode for a logical record, the database is organized 'by logical record'. An index file, called a 'base index' contains different keys, each one identifying a logical record. With each key is associated a pointer indicating the address *in the linkage file* of the start of the linkage chain for the record. The links of this chain contain pointers to the storage file proper (Fig. 3.22).

The storage file consists of fairly large record-blocks (one record per block or page); each block contains general purpose words (or bytes, or half-bytes). The data are stored in compact form, each field or group occupying an area of length as predefined in the dictionary or table, and starting from a predefined address. New data are always stored at the end of the file and noted in the linkage chain in order to become part of a given record. The concept of record description, such as it exists in COBOL or FORTRAN, has therefore disappeared. A logical record can be spread over several blocks, all the parts being linked to each other at the linkage chain level.

Note: Since the storage is performed by a general-purpose method, the value of packing the data using a power-of-2 base is strengthened, thus preserving the independence of the fields. The pointers declared in the structure can be repeated (a group P (6) of six consecutive pointers is valid), or be used to go through the database by different chains (lists) which exist in addition to the linkage chains. It is, however, generally preferable to make them point to the linkage chains, as this allows greater flexibility in storage for adding new fields to the main file.

As for linkage files, it is worthwhile to set aside an overflow area in each block (see section 3.6.3.2).

### 3.6.3.1  Multiple Storage Files
Since the storage is done by a general purpose method of concatenating data, in order to access a particular piece of data we are obliged (in spite of the direct access possible on account of the linkage chain) to transfer a whole block of a

few thousand characters in order to obtain a few useful characters. We can avoid this wastage in volume of memory/disk transfers by using *several* storage files. For example, if 80% of the database volume is made up of 'items' (number, text, quantity, etc.) and 20% of some 600 other pieces of information stored, we use two files:

an 'item' file containing only the GF 'items';
an 'other information' file.

The specialization of storage files often separates the data into groups of *different stability*. We are therefore better able to use the technique of overflow areas in each block by adjusting the block size to the stability of the data in the file. Multiple specialized files therefore provide an interesting possibility for improving performance in accessing the database. This technique does, however, complicate the addressing method used in the linkage chain. It is necessary often to use one linkage file per physical storage file; and to set aside in the 'base' linkage chain (pointed to by the base index and corresponding to the 'other information' file) a pointer to each of the other linkage files to indicate the start of each 'linkage subchain', corresponding to data marked as belonging to the same chain (identifying the same records).

### 3.6.3.3.2 Multiples Indexes

The base index facilitates accesses corresponding to the 'base' key chosen to build the database. It is clear that other rapid access methods are necessary. To achieve this, we build up as many indexes (hierarchical, binary tree, hash code, existence table) as necessary. These indexes (called 'secondary indexes') point the linkage file(s), indicating each time the start of the chain containing the data, or a link corresponding to a group containing the data, or the link of the data itself. Pointing to the 'middle of a chain' can improve search time for the data, but sometimes makes it necessary to go back up the chain using the appropriate pointers in order to find information at higher levels.

### 3.6.3.3.3 Note on Detail Chains D→ and DG→

In general, such a chain represents a structure of 'open item' type. This structure therefore contains a group of header fields and groups of detail fields linked by pointers. When additions of details can happen frequently, we must allow for storage, in (or with) the header, of a pointer indicating the *last* detail. We can thus access this detail without scanning its predecessors, and write in it a pointer to the new 'last detail', when the time comes. This pointer in fact indicates the corresponding link in the linkage chain.

Generally, the structure shown in Fig. 3.23a can be used in all cases of *frequent additions*, whether the database is open content or not. This type of list is called 'FIFO' (First in First Out). In addition, Fig. 3.23b is even more efficient when there are many details and/or many additions. The *last* detail is always inserted at the *beginning* of the list. This type of list is called 'LIFO' (Last In First Out).

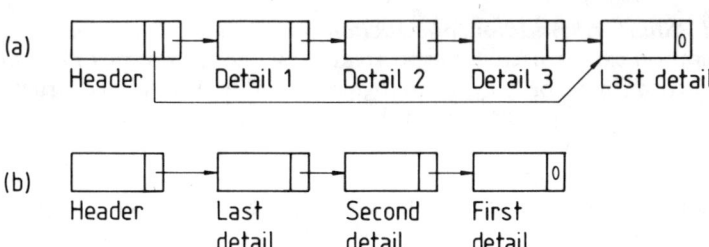

(a) Header | Detail 1 | Detail 2 | Detail 3 | Last detail

(b) Header | Last detail | Second detail | First detail

Fig. 3.23

### 3.6.3.3.4 Use of Existence Tables with Open Content Databases

Existence tables (sometimes called 'inverted' files) have been defined in section 3.3.5.1. It is equally worthwhile to take advantage of their small size with an open content database as with a closed one. But because the logical records of an open content database are variable length and can possibly be spread over several physical records, we cannot simply associate a group of descriptive bits with a logical record without adding a space-taking pointer. We then associate the group of bits with an index (base or secondary) existing elsewhere. Searching for a record having the desired properties therefore involves the following operations:

1. Scanning the existence table.
2. When the bit-group number N indicates a record to be retained, we access record number N of the corresponding index.
3. We find there the address of the record description in the linkage file.
4. We then access the linkage file, and go through the linkage chain searching for the addresses of the required pieces of information.
5. Finally we access the information itself in the main storage file.

### 3.6.3.4 Operations on Open Content Databases

By their very nature, open content databases can be subject to two types of operation:

1. The *'standard' operations* defined in the same way as for non-open content databases (section 3.1): 0, − +, MOD, SEL, RES,
2. The *evolutions*:
   addition/subtraction of fields (or generally of data) of new types, which we will symbolise by +F,
   the creation of chains linking the data with a common characteristic, which we can symbolize by + →,
   the creation of individual access paths or indexes (or hierarchies of indexes), other than the base index previously defined, which we can symbolize by +I.

We describe below the characteristics of these different operations; as far as the standard operations are concerned, we point out only what represents a new aspect due to the 'open' nature of the database.

89

### 3.6.3.4.1 'Standard Addition/Subtraction

This operation can be used either to create a whole record; or *to complete an existing record* (by record, we mean logical record with a defined structure, on creation of the database, located in the base index and having its own linkage chain).

1. *Creation of a whole record.* This operation is similar to its equivalent for databases that are not open content. We must check that the corresponding key in the base index does not exist already, update the base index, create a new linkage chain, update the different secondary indexes and complete the existing chains. For this we use the table of chains and indexes.

2. *Addition of information to an existing record.* Here we are concerned with information whose type is already known, not with new information (which would constitute an evolution of the database). We wish, for example, to add new details to a chain of details, or to add a field already allowed for in the structure but not yet present. We can check the presence of the record and the absence of the information to be added, using the linkage chain; we can then mark in the linkage chain the new information added:

if there is space in the last group of links we can use it;
   if not we can create a new group of links connected to the preceding one by the pointer reserved for this purpose.

We then write the new information in the available space (in the same block or at the end of the file) using the least possible amount of space, adjacent to the last preceding piece of information. We also update the pointers indicating the new first available space (same block or end of file); finally we can update the different chains or indexes described in the table of chains or indexes.

### 3.6.3.4.2 Selection

1. The first difference between selection on an open content database and on other database types results from the presence of the linkage file. Whether or not we use indexes: they point to the linkage file; we cannot guarantee the presence and validity of information until we have checked them in the linkage chain. Since the selection mechanisms are described in the following part of this book, we limit ourselves here to stating that a SEL operation on an open content database is always done in two stages:

   verification in its linkage chain whether or not a given record is a candidate for selection;
   if it is, reading of this record and verification of the data it contains.

2. The second difference between selection operations on open content and non-open content databases results from the considerable amount of information contained in the logical record; when such a record is declared selected, it is not (generally) reasonable to recopy it entirely (by displaying it on a screen or a printer, or writing it in an output selection file).

Generally, we need only a few of the pieces of information in this record; these are the only ones we recopy, and in a custom-defined format described at the time of selection. **This point is of paramount importance; if the database evolves, a previously defined selection continues to give the same results.**

In other words, selection makes the application programs using the database independent with respect to the evolution of the database. This advantage is a determining factor.

3.  The third difference consists of a particular type of selection, navigating along a type of chain (or secondary index). The following sections show how the construction of such a chain (or index) can be made automatic (though costly). Then by using such a chain (or index) we can select (in logical order) several pieces of information such as:

> for each customer, the list of his orders, in relative order of the order number,
> for each account (bookkeeping), the list of transactions.

Of course, as with the 'standard' selection operation, we can obtain partial totals (per chain) or general totals (for all chains combined) and specific fields for the selected records. Since chains (or indexes) are obtained automatically, this permits ordered selections, and simplifies considerably the production of statistics or even the simple interrogation of the database. We can sometimes accept the longer execution time associated with the creation of a special chain (or index) for *a single* statistic or interrogation, since no special program need be written.

*3.6.3.4.3 Addition/Subtraction of Types of Information: +F*
*Addition*: this operation completes the logical data structure, by adding one or several new pieces of information, of any type whatsoever:

GF, F, D →, DG →, or P.

We can first of all complete the definition of the structure:

The updating of the graphical representation and the data
dictionary by the analysts and the database administrator.
The updating of the information description table, by the
appropriate software; if it is powerful enough, this can automatically regenerate the graphical description, the data dictionary and the information description table from *instructions for the evolution of the data table* supplied in a *data description language.*
If appropriate, the updating of the chains and indexes: thus we can represent the existence of chains connecting the new records, or of indexes pointing to them; if one of the new records is a pointer, we indicate it in the description of the relevant chain. We then perform a restructuring operation (RES) on the database, intended to recreate it by leaving space for the new records (refer to 'Restructuring', section 3.6.3.4.6 below).

This structure is then ready to receive the numeric or alphanumeric values to be assigned to the new data; this is done by 'standard' addition or modification operations.

Comment: The software of an open content database is adapted to its openness; this software reads and writes to the database following the record description tables, and through the chains and indexes. Therefore the evolution of the database can take place without the recompilation of the programs that access it: *this point is very important*.

*Subtraction*: this operation works in the same way as addition; instead of creating new descriptive entries in the tables, it merely marks the validity codes of the data items to be deleted. The next restructuring operation physically removes these data items by not copying them from the old version of the database to the new one.

### 3.6.3.4.4 Creation of links: + →

This operation creates a sequence of pointers, interconnecting those records that have a common characteristic. It consists of the following stages:

1. *Definition of the type of link.* By means of the data definition language and/or procedure, we can define the records required for the table of chains and indexes, and the pointers P to the record description table, to the data dictionary and to the graphical representation. We can then actually update the tables.

2. *Definition of the linkage criterion.* This criterion is of the type 'same customer number' or 'same customer number *and* same month'; it consists of a collection of fields F where we connect (using pointers) all the logical records (or GF) that contain the fields with the same values. We point to the linkage file, at the beginning or 'in the middle' of the chain.

3. *Selection.* We can go through the entire database by making use of the linkage file; we keep only those records (or GF) that contain the relevant field(s), that is (or are) in an 'accessible' state that is (not deleted, authorized access). Each time we note, in a work file W, the value(s) of the selected field(s) as well as the address in the linkage file of the link that describes the beginning of the record (or GF) concerned. This process of going through the whole of the database can take considerable time (quite often several hours).

4. *Construction of the chains.* We then sort the work file W according to the values of the fields, to regroup the records that correspond to the same values and thus belonging to the same chain. We can of course concatenate at the end of the sort key field an order criterion (such as date or order number) that produces each chain in the desired order. We merely need to note in W the required auxiliary value (criterion) in the same record as the value of the definition fields of the chain. We then go on to the actual chaining process; we add to each record a pointer field where we write the address of the connecting link of the record that logically follows it in the chain, known thanks to file W. We note this pointer in the linkage chain of the record. If necessary, we note at the beginning and end of each chain the required addresses in the headers file. This process can also take a long time.

The previous process can be automated; this is advantageous in spite of the long execution time. Furthermore, when a chain of pointers is broken it can be used to reconstruct the chain; finally, it can also be used for a restructuring operation.

Note on relational databases: Generally speaking, when we create links or chains through the set of data that make up a database, we divide it into new subsets. The point of view of set and subset manipulation is a totally *different* approach to database management. When the sets of data are considered unordered (records) and ordered (fields within a record) we are in the realm of *relational database management.*

This approach is an application of the theory of sets to database management. The fundamental operations consider sets (called relations, equivalent to our logical files) and comprise intersection, union, join, difference, etc. The advantage of the relational approach over the navigational approach (the approach described above, which implies 'navigating' through the database from one piece of information to the next, using file access methods and linkage techniques) is that no data structure is known by the end-user of the database. The drawbacks are that today we cannot implement *efficient* relational database management systems on existing computers, and that the end-user needs to have a certain ability to understand and use the abstract mathematical concepts involved in set manipulation.

*Note on the storage of pointers P:* To simplify the explanation about the construction of links and chains, we have considered *pointers* (apart from the 'arrows' in D→ and DG→ ) as individual data items; provision has been made, implicitly or explicitly, for their storage in the data storage file. In practice, we usually do things differently; *the pointers are stored in the linkage chain*, even though they are special data items, so they can be accessed by the programs using the database. A link containing a pointer will therefore generally contain:

the data item number of the pointer;
the validity code;
the value of the pointer (in other words, the address it gives).

This simplification is particularly valuable each time that the pointer points to a linkage file (the same file or not)—this is the most frequent case. Thus the end of a chain can be indicated equally by the absence of a chain pointer or by a pointer with a zero address.

### 3.6.3.4.5 Creation of Individual Indexes: +I

1. *Comparison between chains and indexes.* There is a great similarity between an index and a collection of chains as described above. An index is a file (or a hierarchy of files) that *contains* the various pointers associated with the fields (or groups of fields) that have been used to construct the index; on the other hand, a chain stores the pointers with the data, and not in a separate file. An index, particularly a hierarchical index, allows a more rapid search than a given entry in a particular chain, for we can scan through an index more quickly than through a chain; on the other hand, an index is larger and more difficult to update. But fundamentally an index and a collection of chains are two means of achieving the same result, to produce in a given file a particular *order*.

This order is used for rapid searches, statistics, or simply for its own sake (as in the sequence in which sales orders arrive).

2. *Automatic construction of specialized indexes.* The analogy between chains and indexes drawn above implies that their creation processes will be similar; we create an index in the same way as we do a group of chains, except that the chain headers file will be replaced by the sorted work file W. In addition, if justified by the size of W, we create one (or, rarely, two) supplementary file(s) producing a hierarchy that can speed up searches in W. Finally, we use the techniques described in sections 3.3.3. to 3.3.6 in order to make any updating required easier (partially filled blocks, etc.).

### 3.6.3.4.6 Restructuring: RES

As for non-open content databases, the restructuring operation involves the copying of the database in logical order, the reconstruction of the indexes and the removal of the information that has been logically deleted.

However, when the database is open content, we can also:

make any necessary changes to the field lengths, add and
    subtract data types, chains or indexes,
reorder (*Resequence*) the linkage chains.

Field lengths rarely change, but they require such changes as:

an alphanumeric field will be able to contain more (or fewer)
    characters than previously;
a numeric field will (or will not) contain a sign, or will be able to
    contain a different number of digits before or after the decimal point.

During a restructuring operation, we copy the data in the old fields to the new (modified) fields, noting any truncations (negative data items becoming positive when the sign is suppressed, the least significant digits being lost when the field size is reduced).

The additions/subtractions of data types (F, GF, DG→, D→, P) involve (during a restructuring operation) the creation/deletion of the corresponding space:

in the database storage file(s),
in the linkage files.

The reordering of the linkage chains simply means that all logically consecutive chains should also be physically consecutive. This reordering goes with the reordering of the database itself—the data items are arranged in the order (now logical) of the linkage chains.

The restructuring process involves the following stages:

1. Updating the data description tables and the chains and indexes in order to take into account the new data items, chains, indexes, data deletions and length modifications.
2. Sorting the updated or rebuilt base index in the order of the base key (unless, of course it is a hash code index).
3. Copying:

For each key of the base index, we find the corresponding chain in the linkage file. We copy the data field by field into a new storage file, building up the new linkage chain as we go along (stored in the new linkage file). This copying operation is done in the logical order of the chain. We take into account the chains and indexes to be reconstructed—as we come across the data to be used to establish the chains and indexes, we note their values and positions in the work file. The various copying operations (without forgetting the base index) respect the planned block filling factors.

4. Reconstructing the chains and secondary indexes, according to the previously described method for their creation.
5. Updating the documentation: graphical representation of the structure, data dictionary (if it is not produced automatically as a result of stage 1).

The restructuring operation RES has considerable effect upon the search time and the updating time of the database; it regroups together the linkage chains and the data, reducing the number of disk accesses for the searches, and reconstructing the overflow areas. On the other hand, it can require several hours of execution, so it is therefore executed at night or during the weekend.

### 3.6.3.5 Example of a Commercial Database

The example below shows a commercial database for a manufacturer, containing three types of information grouped together for each customer:

the customer parameters (number, name, address, etc.);
the current orders for this customer;
the invoices sent out for this customer and the corresponding different payments made, building up a historical record of the customer's transactions.

In total, there are more than 100 different types of information. As well as the above chains, we have allowed for secondary indexes by order number, and by index number. To speed up searching *by date* (orders, invoices for a given day or a given month), we create special indexes. These are similar to the indexes by order number or invoice number, but they include a date (instead of the order numbers or invoice numbers) and a pointer; they are sorted by date. In the graphical representation (Fig. 3.24–3.27), we have used the COBOL notation to describe the fields:

9 indicates a one-digit field;
99 or 9(2) indicates a two-digit field, etc.;
S9(4) indicates a *signed* four-digit field;

$GF_0$          customer

     — $FG_1$      customer parameters (Fig. 3.25)
     — $DG_2 \rightarrow$    current orders (Fig. 3.26)
     — $DG_3 \rightarrow$    invoices sent out (details and list of payments: history) (Fig. 3.27)

Fig. 3.24   Commercial database (basic structure).

95

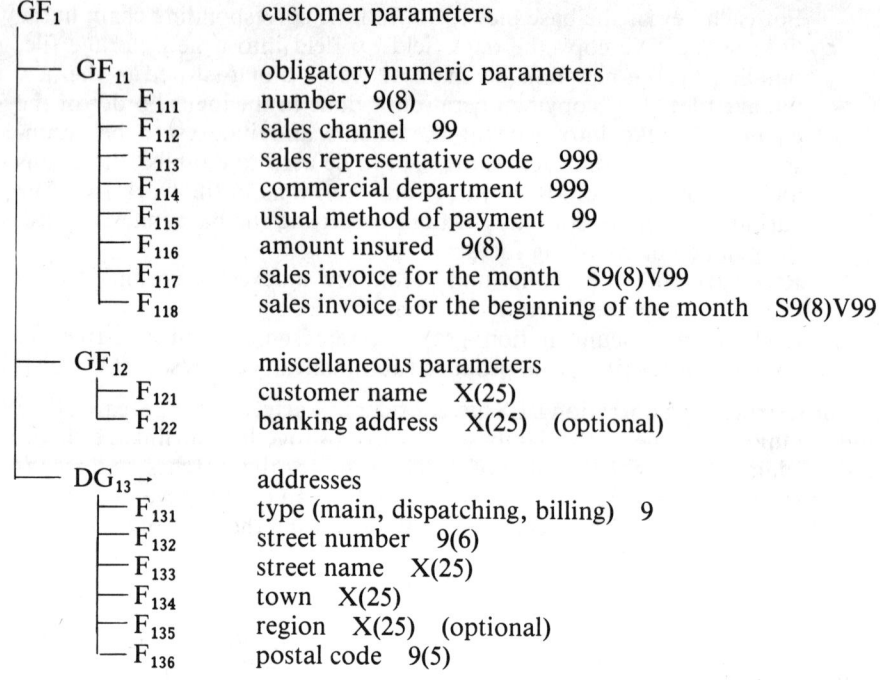

| | | |
|---|---|---|
| GF$_1$ | | customer parameters |
| | GF$_{11}$ | obligatory numeric parameters |
| | F$_{111}$ | number   9(8) |
| | F$_{112}$ | sales channel   99 |
| | F$_{113}$ | sales representative code   999 |
| | F$_{114}$ | commercial department   999 |
| | F$_{115}$ | usual method of payment   99 |
| | F$_{116}$ | amount insured   9(8) |
| | F$_{117}$ | sales invoice for the month   S9(8)V99 |
| | F$_{118}$ | sales invoice for the beginning of the month   S9(8)V99 |
| | GF$_{12}$ | miscellaneous parameters |
| | F$_{121}$ | customer name   X(25) |
| | F$_{122}$ | banking address   X(25)   (optional) |
| | DG$_{13}$→ | addresses |
| | F$_{131}$ | type (main, dispatching, billing)   9 |
| | F$_{132}$ | street number   9(6) |
| | F$_{133}$ | street name   X(25) |
| | F$_{134}$ | town   X(25) |
| | F$_{135}$ | region   X(25)   (optional) |
| | F$_{136}$ | postal code   9(5) |

Fig. 3.25   Detailed structure of GF$_1$ 'customer parameters'

X(25) indicates a text of up to 25 characters.

Note: the database is organized *by customer* (there is one base index per customer). The approximate sizes are:

Number of customers: 300;
Number of current orders: 3000 (170 000 lines);
Number of invoices sent out during the period covered by the history: 9000 (500 000 lines);
Number of payments made: 15 000.

To simplify the answers to certain frequently occurring questions (interrogations, statistics), we have allowed for the following eight logical chains:

    by sales channel (orders, invoices),
    by sales-representative (orders, invoices),
    by commercial department (orders, invoices),
    by family items (orders, invoices)

The pointers are stored in the linkage file.

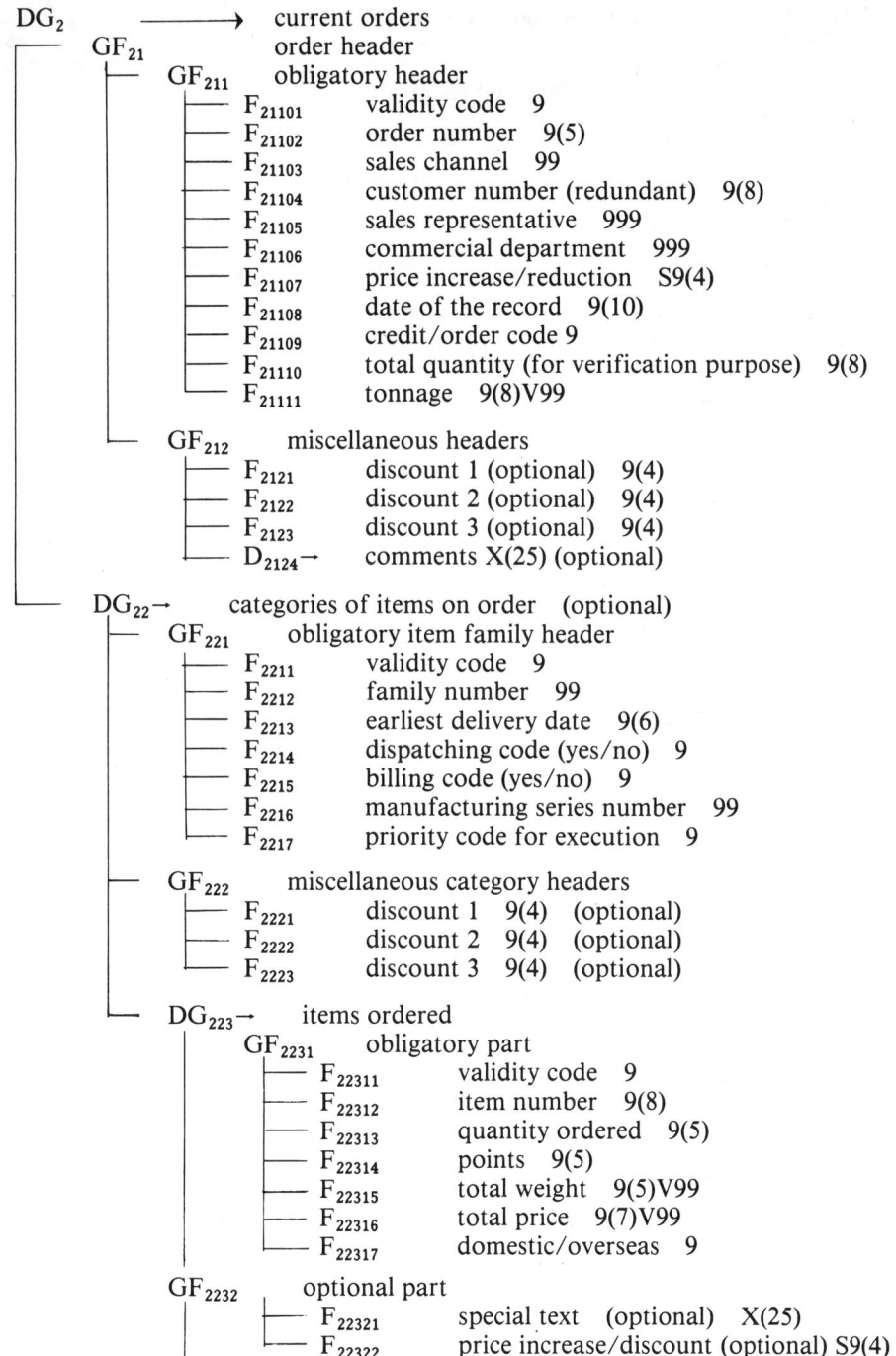

```
DG₂        ─────→    current orders
 ┌─ GF₂₁              order header
 │   ┌─ GF₂₁₁          obligatory header
 │   │   ┌── F₂₁₁₀₁        validity code   9
 │   │   ├── F₂₁₁₀₂        order number    9(5)
 │   │   ├── F₂₁₁₀₃        sales channel   99
 │   │   ├── F₂₁₁₀₄        customer number (redundant)   9(8)
 │   │   ├── F₂₁₁₀₅        sales representative   999
 │   │   ├── F₂₁₁₀₆        commercial department   999
 │   │   ├── F₂₁₁₀₇        price increase/reduction   S9(4)
 │   │   ├── F₂₁₁₀₈        date of the record   9(10)
 │   │   ├── F₂₁₁₀₉        credit/order code 9
 │   │   ├── F₂₁₁₁₀        total quantity (for verification purpose)   9(8)
 │   │   └── F₂₁₁₁₁        tonnage   9(8)V99
 │   │
 │   └─ GF₂₁₂          miscellaneous headers
 │       ┌── F₂₁₂₁         discount 1 (optional)   9(4)
 │       ├── F₂₁₂₂         discount 2 (optional)   9(4)
 │       ├── F₂₁₂₃         discount 3 (optional)   9(4)
 │       └── D₂₁₂₄→        comments X(25) (optional)
 │
 └─ DG₂₂→            categories of items on order   (optional)
     ┌─ GF₂₂₁          obligatory item family header
     │   ┌── F₂₂₁₁         validity code   9
     │   ├── F₂₂₁₂         family number   99
     │   ├── F₂₂₁₃         earliest delivery date   9(6)
     │   ├── F₂₂₁₄         dispatching code (yes/no)   9
     │   ├── F₂₂₁₅         billing code (yes/no)   9
     │   ├── F₂₂₁₆         manufacturing series number   99
     │   └── F₂₂₁₇         priority code for execution   9
     │
     ┌─ GF₂₂₂          miscellaneous category headers
     │   ┌── F₂₂₂₁         discount 1   9(4)   (optional)
     │   ├── F₂₂₂₂         discount 2   9(4)   (optional)
     │   └── F₂₂₂₃         discount 3   9(4)   (optional)
     │
     └─ DG₂₂₃→          items ordered
         GF₂₂₃₁           obligatory part
             ┌── F₂₂₃₁₁        validity code   9
             ├── F₂₂₃₁₂        item number   9(8)
             ├── F₂₂₃₁₃        quantity ordered   9(5)
             ├── F₂₂₃₁₄        points   9(5)
             ├── F₂₂₃₁₅        total weight   9(5)V99
             ├── F₂₂₃₁₆        total price   9(7)V99
             └── F₂₂₃₁₇        domestic/overseas   9
         GF₂₂₃₂           optional part
             ┌── F₂₂₃₂₁        special text   (optional)   X(25)
             └── F₂₂₃₂₂        price increase/discount (optional) S9(4)
```

Fig. 3.26   Detailed structure of DG₂ 'current orders'.

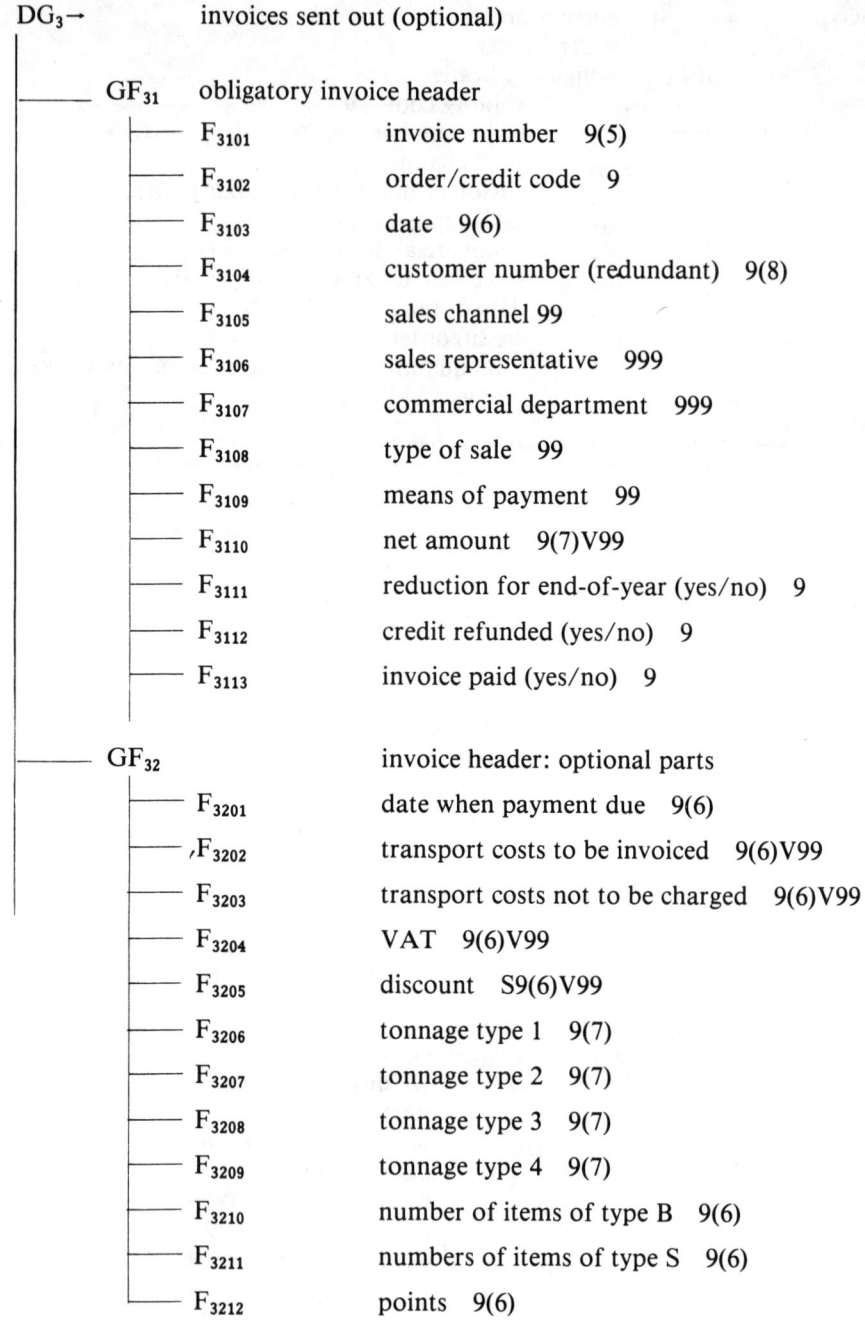

$DG_3 \rightarrow$      invoices sent out (optional)

      $GF_{31}$    obligatory invoice header

         $F_{3101}$      invoice number   9(5)

         $F_{3102}$      order/credit code   9

         $F_{3103}$      date   9(6)

         $F_{3104}$      customer number (redundant)   9(8)

         $F_{3105}$      sales channel 99

         $F_{3106}$      sales representative   999

         $F_{3107}$      commercial department   999

         $F_{3108}$      type of sale   99

         $F_{3109}$      means of payment   99

         $F_{3110}$      net amount   9(7)V99

         $F_{3111}$      reduction for end-of-year (yes/no)   9

         $F_{3112}$      credit refunded (yes/no)   9

         $F_{3113}$      invoice paid (yes/no)   9

      $GF_{32}$               invoice header: optional parts

         $F_{3201}$      date when payment due   9(6)

         $F_{3202}$      transport costs to be invoiced   9(6)V99

         $F_{3203}$      transport costs not to be charged   9(6)V99

         $F_{3204}$      VAT   9(6)V99

         $F_{3205}$      discount   S9(6)V99

         $F_{3206}$      tonnage type 1   9(7)

         $F_{3207}$      tonnage type 2   9(7)

         $F_{3208}$      tonnage type 3   9(7)

         $F_{3209}$      tonnage type 4   9(7)

         $F_{3210}$      number of items of type B   9(6)

         $F_{3211}$      numbers of items of type S   9(6)

         $F_{3212}$      points   9(6)

Fig. 3.27   Detailed structure of $DG_3$ 'invoices sent out'

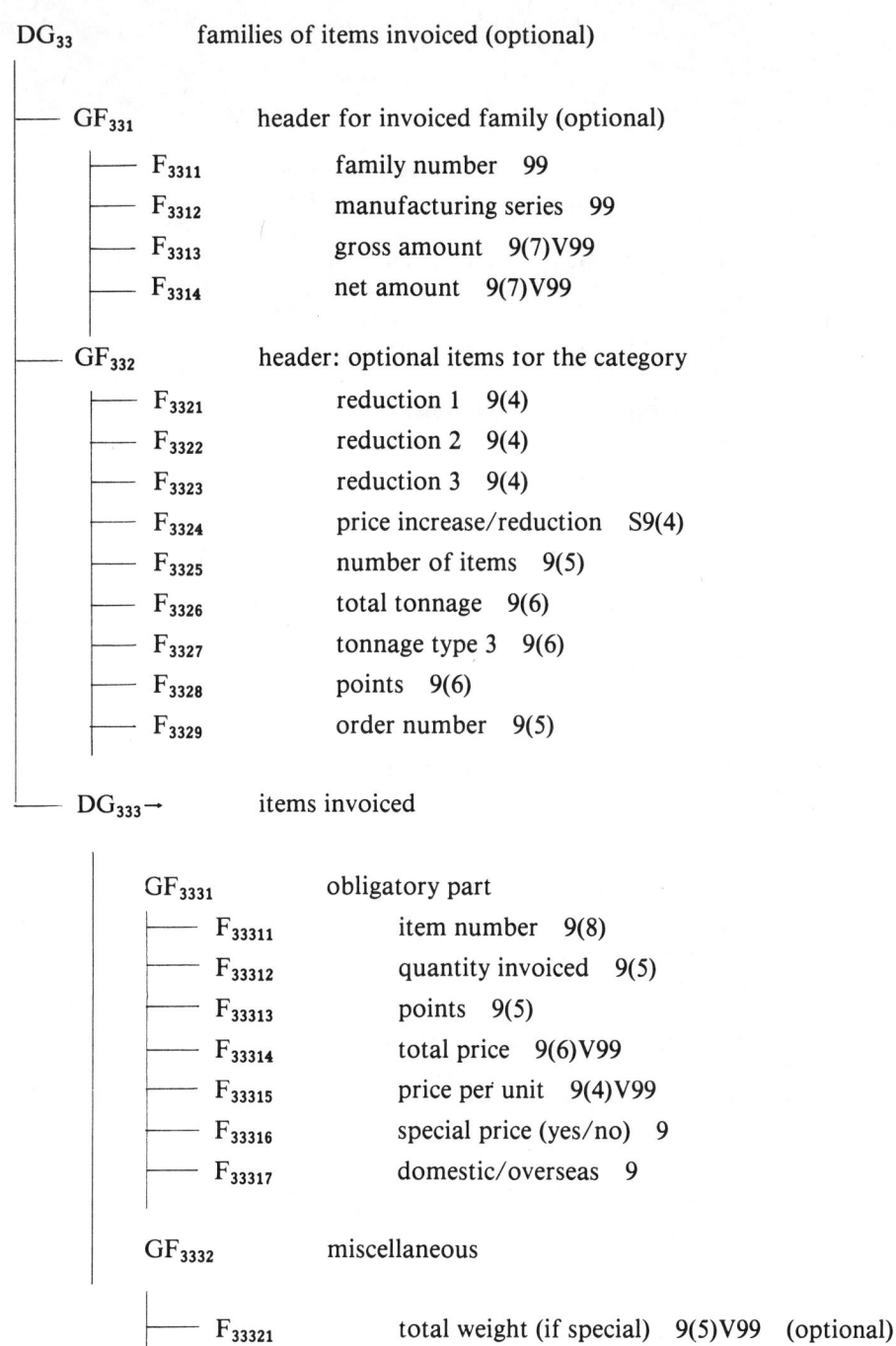

DG$_{33}$        families of items invoiced (optional)

    GF$_{331}$        header for invoiced family (optional)

       F$_{3311}$        family number   99
       F$_{3312}$        manufacturing series   99
       F$_{3313}$        gross amount   9(7)V99
       F$_{3314}$        net amount   9(7)V99

    GF$_{332}$        header: optional items for the category

       F$_{3321}$        reduction 1   9(4)
       F$_{3322}$        reduction 2   9(4)
       F$_{3323}$        reduction 3   9(4)
       F$_{3324}$        price increase/reduction   S9(4)
       F$_{3325}$        number of items   9(5)
       F$_{3326}$        total tonnage   9(6)
       F$_{3327}$        tonnage type 3   9(6)
       F$_{3328}$        points   9(6)
       F$_{3329}$        order number   9(5)

    DG$_{333}$→        items invoiced

       GF$_{3331}$        obligatory part

       F$_{33311}$        item number   9(8)
       F$_{33312}$        quantity invoiced   9(5)
       F$_{33313}$        points   9(5)
       F$_{33314}$        total price   9(6)V99
       F$_{33315}$        price per unit   9(4)V99
       F$_{33316}$        special price (yes/no)   9
       F$_{33317}$        domestic/overseas   9

       GF$_{3332}$        miscellaneous

       F$_{33321}$        total weight (if special)   9(5)V99   (optional)
       F$_{33322}$        price increase/discount   S9(4)   (optional)

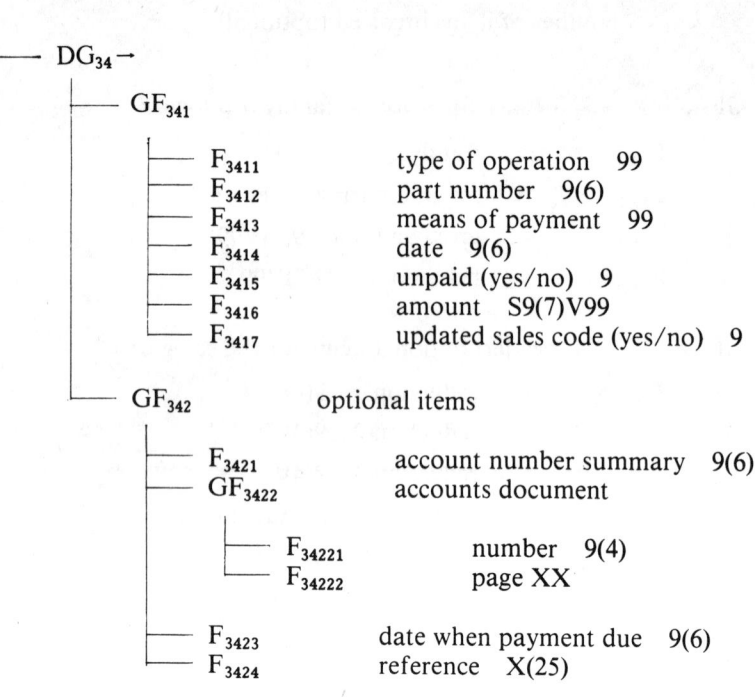

```
└─ DG₃₄ →
   ├─── GF₃₄₁
   │        ├─── F₃₄₁₁          type of operation   99
   │        ├─── F₃₄₁₂          part number   9(6)
   │        ├─── F₃₄₁₃          means of payment   99
   │        ├─── F₃₄₁₄          date   9(6)
   │        ├─── F₃₄₁₅          unpaid (yes/no)   9
   │        ├─── F₃₄₁₆          amount   S9(7)V99
   │        └─── F₃₄₁₇          updated sales code (yes/no)   9
   └─── GF₃₄₂          optional items
            ├─── F₃₄₂₁          account number summary   9(6)
            ├─── GF₃₄₂₂         accounts document
            │       ├─── F₃₄₂₂₁          number   9(4)
            │       └─── F₃₄₂₂₂          page XX
            ├─── F₃₄₂₃          date when payment due   9(6)
            └─── F₃₄₂₄          reference   X(25)
```

### 3.6.3.5.1 *Choice of Storage Files*

Considering the structure and size of the information to be stored, we can make the following remarks:

1.  There is a strong similarity between the items ordered and the items invoiced, and it is easy to find a *fixed-length* record format able to store the information described for one item or the other.
2.  The order lines (items ordered) and the invoice lines (items invoiced) comprise—by far—most of the volume of data to be stored and manipulated.
3.  The simplicity of the information stored and the stability of the production encourage the choice of *an 'items' file with fixed structure* to store the item-lines, with no linkage file. To connect an item-line with such and such an order or invoice we use:

    a pointer *towards* this file, indicating the start of an item-chain, and stored with the rest of the order or invoice in another file;

    forward pointers, making up an item-chain, linking each item to the next in the family of items;

    the existence (redundant but justified by the need for safety in the case of loss of pointers) in each item record of: order number or invoice number, family number, and type code:

    0 for a deleted record
    1 for an 'order' record
    2 for an 'invoice' record.

4. Apart from a reference of two characters, which we can store in numeric coded form, all the texts have the same format. They can therefore be stored in a 'text file' of fixed format, without a linkage file, where the connection to such and such a customer, order or invoice will be made by a pointer. This structure is the same as the preceding item-file, except that it is useless to allow for the chaining of the texts.

5. It is worthwhile to separate the text from the rest of the data because: searches are made on numeric data and not on these texts, and the files to be searched are much shorter if these texts are absent;
   a text-file with fixed format is easier to manipulate during read–write operations than the file 'where everything is crammed in together' (below) and where the data are stored in variable format. The need for safety leads us to set aside in the text-file some *codes* allowing us to off set any possible loss of pointers: type of text (the field number is sufficient); and original item (or payment) and order (or invoice).

6. The opening of the database requires that the other information be gathered into the same file with a floating structure, called a 'holdall', described by a linkage file which will be pointed to by the base index, sorted by customer number. Given the number of customers, this index must have two hierarchical levels (one index per block, one detailed index).

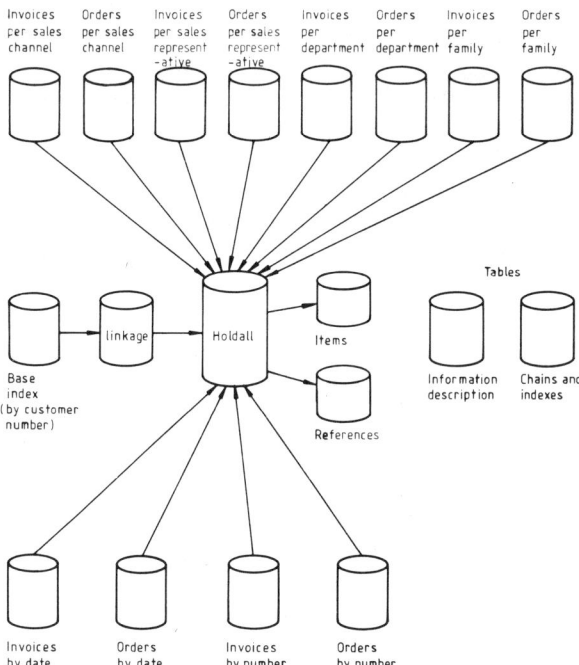

Fig. 3.28   Open content commercial database: physical files. Note: the arrows represent pointers.

Taking these remarks into account, the chains and secondary indexes allowed for elsewhere, the following breakdown into files is made (Fig. 3.28).

### 3.6.3.5.2 *Notes on Programming the Fundamental Operations on this Open Content Database*

*Storage of optional data*

1. When a data item is optional, it is necessary to allow (in the linkage chain) for the storage of its descriptive link, *whether the data exists or not*, when storing the GF to which it is attached. In effect, if we omit it and have to create it later, this could prove to be impossible without recopying the whole linkage chain; and we have seen that it is convenient to reserve this type of operation (which is costly in terms of machine time) to the rare operations of restructuring or evolution. This important point goes beyond the scope of the example.

   In practice, if we suppose that, in the linkage chain:

   a field number occupies three digits,
   the validity code occupies one digit,
   three pointers occupy 21 digits,

   we need more space to store a descriptive link (25 digits) than for any other numeric data stored in the 'holdall' file. We can therefore decide to consider all the optional data of type F as obligatory. The pointers indicate (in the linkage file): the starting position of the description for the given GF (if it is a GF); and the DG→ following (if it is a DG→).

2. As far as the short optional fields attached to the *items* in the example are concerned, it is best to allow for their systematic storage, with no necessity to store zeros there. This is a slight snag; the alternative is to store them in the holdall file (which means they have to be described in the linkage file and attached to an item record), and this is much more costly.

3. Finally, the optional alphanumeric fields are taken up in a pointer to the text file, and set to zero if absent. These notes allow us to map the logical structure of the data to the following schematic storage structure (Fig. 3.29).

This structure shows the field numbers and positions that we can find in the linkage file; there are much fewer fields than the hundred-odd at the start. If we notice now that we have allowed for the linkage of the ordered items to each other by a chain, as well as for the invoiced items, we can set aside in the headings $GF_{221}$ and $GF_{321}$ a pointer to the corresponding physical addresses in the item-file; this pointer contains zero if the item is absent in the family in question. The structure then becomes as shown in Fig. 3.30.

The number of fields at the start (greater than 100) has been divided by 10 for the linkage file. This conciseness guarantees a rapid read of the linkage file. The speed of the read operation is further increased by the 'tree' structure of each linkage chain that is stored. In order to represent this 'chain tree' structure, we are concerned neither with the size of the records and blocks of the linkage file, nor with the assignment of links to a given group, nor with the interrelationship of the groups to form a logical linkage chain.

We represent the links of a given customer linkage chain by depicting one link

102

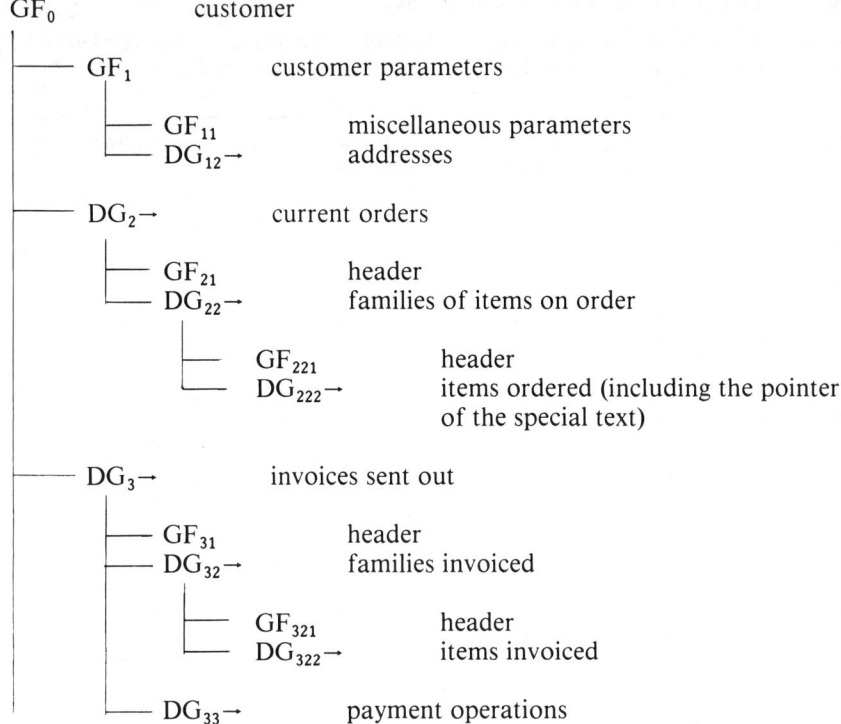

Fig. 3.29   Schematic storage structure (first reduction).

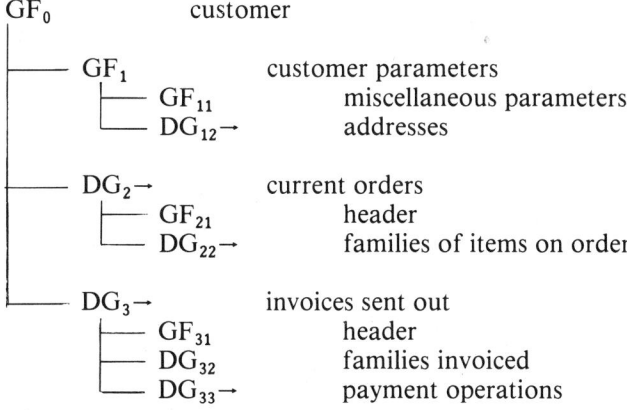

Fig. 3.30   Schematic storage structure (second reduction).

**Table 3.7  Linkage Chain of First Customer: Start**

Note: The letters represent pointers to the holdall file. The creation order was: Order 1, Invoice 1, Order 2, Addition of a category to the invoice 1, Invoice 2.

| Link | Level | Data item number | Pointer 1 (subdivision) | Pointer 2 (sequence DG→) | Comments |
|------|-------|------------------|-------------------------|--------------------------|----------|
| 1  | 0 | 0  | 2  | —  | |
| 2  | 1 | 1  | 5  | —  | |
| 3  | 1 | 2  | 7  | 12 | |
| 4  | 1 | 3  | 9  | 18 | |
| 5  | 2 | 11 | A  | —  | |
| 6  | 2 | 12 | B  | —  | |
| 7  | 2 | 21 | C  | —  | |
| 8  | 2 | 22 | D  | 0  | one single family |
| 9  | 2 | 31 | E  | —  | |
| 10 | 2 | 32 | F  | 17 | |
| 11 | 2 | 33 | G  | 0  | One single payment |
| 12 | 1 | 2  | 13 | 0  | only two codes |
| 13 | 2 | 21 | H  | —  | |
| 14 | 2 | 22 | I  | 15 | |
| 15 | 2 | 22 | J  | 16 | |
| 16 | 2 | 22 | K  | 0  | Three families |
| 17 | 2 | 32 | L  | 0  | Two families |
| 18 | 1 | 3  | 19 | 0  | Two invoices |
| 19 | 2 | 31 | M  | —  | |
| 20 | 2 | 32 | N  | 22 | |
| 21 | 2 | 33 | P  | 31 | Several payments |

To simplify the exploration, we associate with each link three explanatory pieces of information not stored in the database:

per line, assuming furthermore that we know how to store the links physically, how to connect them into groups and how to connect the groups into chains (Table 3.7).

   its logical position within the chain,
   the level of the data item described there,
   a comment.

The (stored) pointer 1 gives either the physical position in the holdall file if it concerns an F, GF, D→, or DG→ that is not subdivided in turn into data items described in the linkage file, or the physical position in the linkage file where the subdivision starts.

The (stored) pointer 2 points to the data item that follows in the same logical chain. It is unused when the link does not have a logical chain header, and set to zero when the corresponding DG→ is last of the chain.

The (stored) pointer 3 to be used for extending the chain ( + F) is not represented; its value is always 0 when there is no extension.

### 3.6.3.5.3 Modules that Search the Linkage File

The basic operations SEL, MOD, + − , RES, involve searches in the linkage file. These searches use the following subprograms, called 'search modules'.

1.  *'One-step search' module*

    Input data: start position in a linkage chain, number of data item to be found.

    Output data: end position in the linkage chain (zero if the data item has not been found); address stored in the pointer associated with the item found.

*Processing*: As a rule, the start position is always the GF or DG→ that contains the data item of the searched number, if the item is in fact present. Starting from this position, the module runs through the linkage chain until it finds the data item, the end of the chain or a data item of a level different from that of the searched item. In the last two cases, it gives the reply 'not found'. If the searched item is a DG→:

> if the starting point is not a DG→ of the type searched for, look
>> for the first DG→ of the type required, as above;
> if the starting point is a DG→ of the type searched for, the
>> following one (or zero) is given, thanks to the associated pointer.

The module is called 'one-step' because the search starts from an item of level $N$ in order to find an item of level $N + 1$, or follows a chain DG→.

Comment. In general, this module need only find a GF or a DG→ (and not an F or a D→) in the linkage file; it is not concerned with the values corresponding to the searched data items, for it does not access the holdall file. It uses the data description table to find the required item or group item that contains it.

2.  *Tree-search' module.*

    Input/output data: The same as for the 'one-step' search module, with in addition on output, the stack of search steps used (see below).

*Processing*. This module starts off by deciding (due to the data description table) on the step-by-step sequences of searches that are required (with the help of the 'one-step' module) to go from the first data item to the last. It then 'runs through' the linkage file using the successive 'step-by-step' searches. At each of these searches it notes the path followed (the sequence of 'one-step' starting points, building up a 'step stack'. When a search is unsuccessful, it goes back (with the help of the stack) and starts again by trying to go back as little as possible within the stack. When it meets the first item of the required type, it stops and gives the reply: 'found'.

Comment. This module preserves the step stack from one search to the next and can reuse it in order to keep advancing. We can (if we like) supply the module with a 'readymade' step stack, which it can use as required for a given search. The module allows us to start from any level A in order to reach any level B, where $B > A$.

### 3.6.3.5.4 Selection Method for the Database

Once we have specified a collection of search criteria, we have to: find the logical

105

records containing the data governed by the above criteria; and compare the values in the files with those of the criteria to decide whether or not to keep the data.

The method outlined below tackles this problem.

1.   We make a list of the data items used in the criteria, noting those that are governed by an index (base, secondary or belonging to a table of chain 'heads' and 'tails').

If no index comes to light, the method is very simple: we go through the database from start to finish, relying on the database index.

If a single index is found, we use it to go through the database. If this index is a table of chain heads and tails, we first of all search it for the 'correct' chain head, then we follow the chain in the linkage file.

If several indexes are found, we search the one with the highest level data item criterion, and use it as above.

Comment: We should check—when using an index—if an existence table suitable for the planned selection is associated with the index in question. Such a table would undoubtedly avoid having to search in the linkage file. This important point applies generally, even though existence tables are not used in this example.

2.   When a 'guiding' index has been chosen, the search through the database is done using the 'tree-search' module in the following way. The data items governed by criteria are arranged in increasing order of level, taking care to construct several groups that reflect the structure of the database.

*Example 3.14*: Let us suppose that we have to find a customer entry for which:

a parameter of $GF_{111}$ is given,
a parameter of $GF_{21}$ is given,
a parameter of $GF_{31}$ is given,
two parameters of $GF_{321}$ are given.

The order to be established is:

$$(GF_{111})(GF_{21})(GF_{31}\ GF_{321})$$

In total, in the database of this example, we can construct three data groups, linked to $GF_1$, $DG_2 \rightarrow$ and $DG_3 \rightarrow$ respectively. Each group is divided (if appropriate) into subgroups: $GF_1$ into $GF_{11}$ and $DG_{12}$, $DG_2 \rightarrow$ into $GF_{21}$, $D_{22} \rightarrow$ and $DG_{23} \rightarrow$ etc. These groups are in turn subdivided, etc.

We then call the 'tree-search' module to find the first data item of the first group, and we check in the holdall file to see if it is the required item. If this is the case, we look for the second item of the first group etc. If the criteria associated with the data items of the first groups are satisfied, we look at those of the second group, etc.

### 3.6.3.5.5 *Addition of Descriptor Links to a Linkage Chain*

We have seen how, thanks to the 'one-step' and 'tree-search' modules, we can go quickly through a linkage chain. We now indicate how we can build it. To simplify the explanation, we rely on the example, although the described procedure is general and goes beyond the scope of the example (see Figures 3.30 and Table 3.7 above).

At its initial creation, as after a restructuring operation, each linkage chain contains (Fig. 3.30): one instance of the data descriptor links $GF_0$, $GF_1$; and at least one instance of the links describing the other data items.

The order of storing these various links is as follows (see Table 3.7). We store link $GF_0$, which becomes the first link in the linkage chain. In the 'pointer 1' field of the link, we indicate address 2, which means that the subdivision (into $GF_1$, $DG_2 \rightarrow$, $DG_3 \rightarrow$) of $GF_0$ is stored starting at address 2. Address 2 is *absolute* and designates a numbering of the links independent of their grouping in physical records. This numbering is physical, and the chain given as an example is the first, since it begins at link 1. In link 2, we store $GF_1$ and (since the three items $GF_1$, $DG_2 \rightarrow$, $DG_3 \rightarrow$ take the links 2, 3, 4) the first available space is 5; we indicate this value in 'pointer 1' of link 2. This means that the subdivision ($GF_{11}$, $DG_{12} \rightarrow$) begins at 5. In link 3, we store $DG_2 \rightarrow$ and put in pointer 1 address 7, where the description ($GF_{21}$, $D_2 \rightarrow$) of $DG_2$ begins. In 'pointer 2', we put the number of the link where the description of the second logical entry of chain $DG_2 \rightarrow$ (second order) will begin. In link 4, we store $DG_3 \rightarrow$, etc.

The creation (or the addition of new orders $DG_2 \rightarrow$, invoices $DG_3 \rightarrow$ or 'pieces' of orders or invoices $DG_{22} \rightarrow$, $DG_{32} \rightarrow$, $DG_{33} \rightarrow$) is always done towards the bottom of the file:

either by placing the new links in the last group of links of the
    linkage chain in question, if space exists,
or by creating a new group of links, which we connect to the
    previous one by a pointer (forward or both forward and backward), then
    by placing the new links there.

Assuming that the algorithm that writes in a group and creates a group in the linkage file is automatic, the calculation of the pointers 1 and 2 is done by means of a *stack*.

# CHAPTER 4

# Database Development Techniques

The aim of this chapter is to indicate some principles which are useful to know when developing a database management system. These principles have proved themselves both simple to understand and easy to put into practice.

## 4.1 GENERAL PRINCIPLES

### 4.1.1 Identifying the Fundamental Operations

When designing a database it is very important to identify clearly the fundamental operations defined in sections 3.1 and 3.6.3.4 of Chapter 3. These are summarized in Table 4.1.

**Table 4.1**

| Symbol | Definition |
| --- | --- |
| 0 | Initial file creation |
| − + | Deletion and addition of records (closed databases) or parts of records (open databases) |
| MOD | Modification of the value stored in a given field |
| SEL | Selection (searching and retrieving) of information satisfying selection criteria |
| RES | Database restructuring: deletion of destroyed information, logical reordering, chain and index restructuring |
| +F | Addition and deletion of types of fields (F, GF, D→, DG→, P) |
| + → | Creation of groups of chains which link common information |
| +I | Creation of special indexes of access paths |

This identification process consists of categorizing each proposed functional creation, search or update operation as a function of the fundamental operations of the above table. We must try to avoid the use of vague terms such as 'updating'. As an example, 'updating' when related to inventory management can mean:

modification of the stock of one or more items;
creation of new items;
deletion of items;
sorting (restructuring) of the item file after the creation or deletion of items.

We see that it is dangerous to use a general program for both item modification and additions/deletions. It is better to identify and separate those operations for which the logical processes are different.

Fundamental operations have precise meanings which depend on the type of database (master file, history file, open item file). In order not to confuse the MOD operation with the − + operation, remember that MOD does not create information (whereas + does) and that − + does not change information but adds or deletes it. Thus addition of new details to linked information is of the − + type, whereas changing a value in a history record (only allowed for correction of errors) is of the MOD type.

### 4.1.2 The Nucleus of a Database

Associated with the fundamental operations identified above is a series of processing units which perform the desired actions, and which have *exclusive access to the database* (exclusivity further justified as the 'window' principle). These processing units can be either programs (in the broadest sense of the word) or specialized subprograms; either they will be compiled together with the user's application programs, or a compiled version will be loaded with each program execution, or link-edit will be used.

The database nucleus is the set of programs and subprograms which create, maintain and search a database. We can see that whatever the subprograms constituting the nucleus, the use of a database requires that there be a program associated with each one of the fundamental operations. So we have:

a 'zero' program (initial creation);
a 'minus–plus' program (deletion and addition of records);
a 'modifications' program, etc.

We can represent these conceptual programs as a series of satellites surrounding a database (Fig. 4.1). In practice it often happens that several programs are necessary to perform certain fundamental operations (− +, MOD, RES). For example a closed database accessed in batch mode from cards will require programs and files as shown in Fig. 4.2 below.

Finally, to clarify the concept of the nucleus of a database, Fig. 4.3 shows the programs which make up the nucleus of the commercial open database from section 3.6.3.5. of Chapter 3.

We notice here the existence of a 'data manipulation' monitor. The function of this program is to perform the required fundamental operations which are initiated by a 'data manipulation language'; after analysis and validation of the required operations, this master program initiates the necessary programs that

109

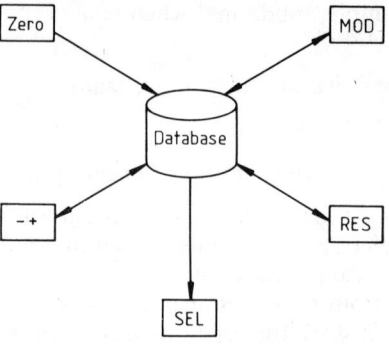

Fig. 4.1    Programs forming the nucleus of a closed database.

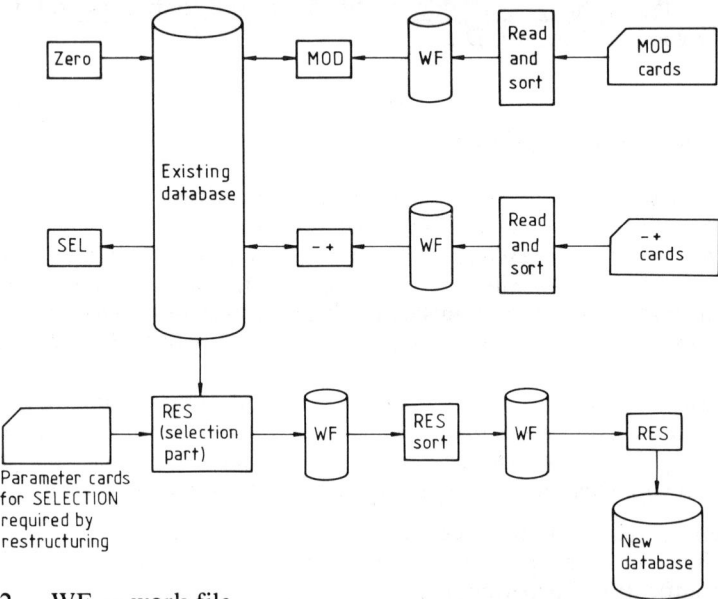

Fig. 4.2    WF = work file.

are executed under its control. Apart from the SEL program (for which output can be sent either to a file or a lineprinter) the various control states, work files, etc. have not been included. The diagram, although more detailed, would have become unclear. Moreover, in an online processing environment, which is common for open databases intended for retrieval, more programs would have had to be added.

### 4.1.3 Three Important Features: Accessibility, Generality, Flexibility

During the life of a database, from the perfecting of the programs and subpro-

110

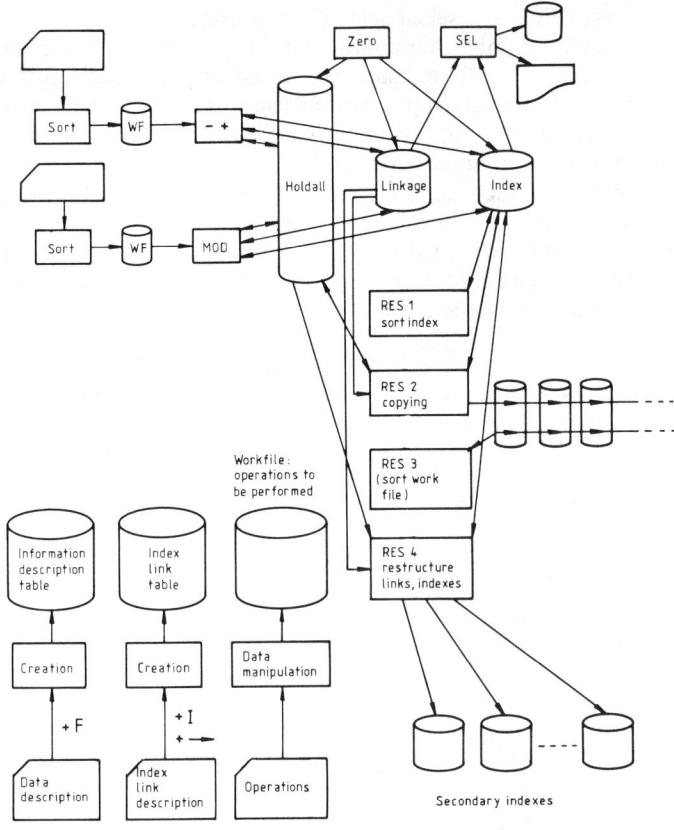

Fig. 4.3    Nucleus of the open commercial database.

grams of the nucleus to the daily use, we find that there are three very important properties, those of accessibility, generality and flexibility.

### 4.1.3.1    Accessibility

refers to the capability of access for storing (write) or retrieving (read) any data field with a defined identity, no matter how small or large. It is as though, in a file consisting of 100 000 cards, we wanted to be able to modify any defined field of a given card, or to retrieve it once the attributes of the card that contains the information have been described. Without accessibility it is necessary to manipulate whole groups of data that are often very large. For example, in order to modify the house number of a customer record consisting of 24 fields, it is necessary to destroy and recreate the whole record.

### 4.1.3.2    Generality

refers to the capability of accessing *all* information to retrieve or modify it. Thus the selection program must be able to retrieve any numeric or alphabetic piece of

111

information according to a set of selection criteria.

Apart from codes of only a few characters in length, alphabetic information is in general quite unreliable. The accuracy of a name or of an address is frequently questionable, and often a given piece of information is shifted in order to centre it within its allocated field. It must also be possible to select information based on numeric and short alphanumeric fields.

The way in which such general selection programs function is described below. We shall note here only the implications of the principle of generality concerning selection criteria: Information selection from a database is defined by a set of criteria. We find that a maximum of ten selection criteria is almost always adequate. Each of the criteria takes the form

<field number> [(index)] <operation> <test value>

Where [(index)] indicates the (optional) index of a field when the field has several occurrences (DIMENSION in FORTRAN, OCCURS in COBOL), <operator> indicates one of the following relational operators

    <less than
<  =less than or equal to
    =equal to
>  =greater than or equal to
    >greater than
<  >not equal to

<test value> represents a numeric or alphabetic constant.

The set of criteria does not necessarily have to be linked to form a single statement. For example the OR in the following statement could be omitted and two separate selections used:

(field # 225 < 13) OR (field # 64 = 12.5)

We find very often that complex selection criteria lead to complicated logical expressions such as (C1 AND C2 AND C3) OR (C1 AND C4) AND (C6 OR C7) and these can lend to wrong selections; users who are not familiar with formal logic are unable to construct correctly their selection criteria and do not exploit to the full the facilities provided. In extreme cases an answer is obtained that does not correspond exactly to the question intended. We could therefore make do with sets of criteria implicity related by AND operations, and ask several questions when necessary.

On the other hand we find that a *different* type of selection described below, is useful. Here we are concerned with a selection where the criteria are defined in the following form:

<field number> [(index)] <operation> <group>

The operation is either 'belongs to' or 'does not belong to' and the group is the name of a file containing a series of constants ('set'). For example we should combine a criterion of the first kind: 'Invoice for February' with a criterion of the second type "representative code belongs to the set {0, 12, 114, 225}.

The first type of criterion describes the state of belonging to an interval. The second type is equivalent to the notion of OR but can be introduced and manipulated without resorting to complex logical expressions. Storing the set in a file has two advantages:

The set consists of as many elements as needed, and can make up an array that can be stored for use in subsequent processing.

The method of creating, storing and coding the file can be standardized independently of the database. Thus for example all the elements can be coded on cards in columns 1 to 12 with one card per element. One program is enough to process the cards. They can be read, sorted and stored on disk in the form of a standard format table file. It is possible to create as many table files as described, or to use a single multitable file. Generally speaking, the use of sets in selection is a major step towards *relational databases*. It is the author's experience that the use of sets, as described above, can be easily understood by everybody. This is definitely not the case with most other concepts of relational database management.

The principle of generality equally implies selection on *totals*. For example, in an invoice history file containing all the invoices sent out during the year, we might, perhaps, want to select all customers having a total billed amount for dairy products greater than £5000. If each customer record contains the 'total dairy products', and the database is structured customer by customer, the problem is reduced to one of simple selection. In general, though, this is not so. We shall see below in this chapter (section 4.2.4) an extension to the idea of selection that allows us to solve this type of problem.

Last but not least, the principle of generality implies miscellaneous capabilities such as:

the possibility of *obtaining* COUNTS ('how many customers live abroad?');
the possibility of *selecting* on counts ('how many customers have over ten invoices for less than $5000 total?') or selecting on the result of arithmetic expressions;
the availability of the date and time of the last update, for each individual record, or for the entire database;
the availability of database usage statistics, by user identification, data element accessed, computer resources used, errors, etc.

### 4.1.3.3 Flexibility

is a feature that refers to the ease of use and evolution of a database. The design of a database, the choice of specifications for the modules making up the nucleus, the distribution of information between open holdall files and fixed format files, influences what can be done on a database, and how it will be done. There are several important points to note here: for instance, all databases, whatever their type and degree of openness need a nucleus of modules allowing the fundamental operations. The omission of a module (RES or MOD for example) is only rarely possible. Even history databases require a MOD module in order to be able to correct errors caused by programs, wrong data or faulty manipulations.

It is advisable to write general programs which will not be affected by database evolution. Thus for example, we must provide for the automatic construction of new chains and indexes that may be initiated simply by the data manipulation language. A selection module can be created capable of manipulating *all present or future* chains and indexes without recompilation. This ambitious attitude is easily justified in the same way that the programming of the nucleus seems difficult only at first glance. It requires order, care and a modular approach, but not the work of a genius. The generality will be limited only by economic considerations. Flexibility and openness are more expensive than a simple rigid system. We shall make sure that the intended lifetime of the database and its planned use and development can justify the level of flexibility chosen.

It is advisable to design access methods, or data description and manipulation languages, that are simple to understand and use. From experience we find that simplicity helps in avoiding errors and is therefore more important than power.

### 4.1.4 Unifying the Processing Procedures: Sample Data Manipulation Language

When daily use of the computer involves several (even a large number of) databases or distinct files, the number of creation, maintenance, selection, restructuring and evolution programs can be considerable. Whenever possible, we shall identify for each file or database the programs that make up the beginning of each chain of programs to bring a fundamental operation into use. These programs are often ones that read cards or tapes with the intent of sorting, when we are referring to creation/maintenance. When referring to selection/restructuring/evolution, these are monitor programs that interpret, initiate and supervise operations expressed in data manipulation language or data description language.

Each of the two types of progams is in general followed by one or more programs that carry on the desired operation specific to the database or file being used. These specific programs can be run automatically at the end of the execution of the first program in the sequence that executes the operation in question. Each program in the sequence can be initiated automatically at the end of execution of the preceding one. From the point of view of program use, since successive programs are run without specific manipulation (loading/unloading tapes, reading parameter cards, etc.) the process is executed as though:

the same types of function are associated with every file or database, that is, zero, $+ -$, MOD, SEL, RES, $+F$, $+\rightarrow$, $+I$;
a separate program must be run for each function.

Thus we end up with a unification of methods of use that proves to be very useful. The following example of unified management of several databases illustrates such a unification designed for the dozen or so permanent databases and permanent files used by an average company on an average computer system.

*Example 4.1* Each database is given a six-letter name, which is punched in columns 1 to 6 on a card. Following this, the names of eight programs (of six letters each) describing the beginning of sequences of fundamental operations

114

are punched. The deck of cards called 'database cards' is loaded via a control program LOADDB which creates the file FILEDB (Fig. 4.4).

A program called 'MASTER' (Fig. 4.5) reads the file FILEDB and receives execution instructions via the operator's console (keyboard) in the form

'DB name' 'instruction to execute'

(For example CUSTOMER – +): The program – + of the 'CUSTOMER' database is then run. This program checks the validity of the requested operations, the existence of the database. It makes sure that the database is on-line, that it is the correct version, and that the files are not being used by another program that could cause a conflict, etc. When the required operation is selection, MASTER must make sure that the data selection instructions are valid. These instructions are presented by using, for example, the 'SELECT' cards.

MASTER checks the validity of the selection criteria—field number, operator, test value—by comparing them with a table containing field numbers: the *data dictionary* DATADIC. For each database, this dictionary contains a list of field numbers. For each field it contains the data type

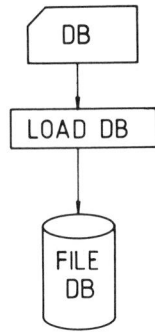

Fig. 4.4

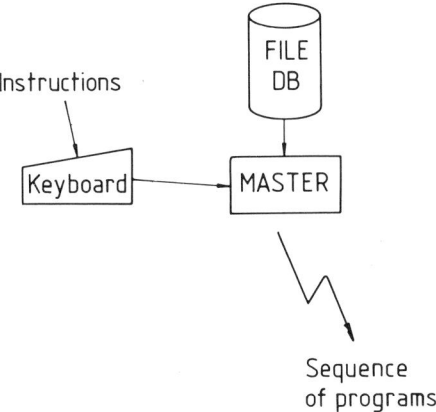

Fig. 4.5

(alphanumeric/numeric), and an indication as to whether or not the data can be used in selection criteria, totalled, etc. (see Chapter 3, section 3.6.3.1).

If everything is all right, the selection program for the required database is run by MASTER, and sends a translation of the SELECT criteria to the database by using a special file called 'CRITERIA', for example (Fig. 4.6).

This example shows how simple it is to group together permanent databases and files, and to unify the initiation of fundamental operations. The systematic nature of this approach is very effective in reducing the number of file-handling errors.

The data manipulation can be summarized for this case by the following concepts:

database or file name;
operation (one of the eight functions 0, $-+$, SEL, MOD, RES, $+F$, $+\rightarrow$, $+I$);
selection language.

Since the associated syntax for concepts 1 and 2 is easy to understand, we shall now continue with this example and describe a possible selection language in detail.

### 4.1.4.1 Selection Language—Language Objectives

This language is used to describe:

Selection criteria (SEL); the set of criteria, comparing fields with reference values, is used to define a sub-set of records from the database in question to satisfy the given criteria.
The fields belonging to selected records, and which must be added up (TOT for 'TOTAL').
The type of output (OUT) required: S = statistics, V = VDU, F = file, P = paper. The 'S' output (statistics) will produce a curve or a histogram on the VDU (see section 4.2.4 below). The 'V' output (default option), 'F' and P

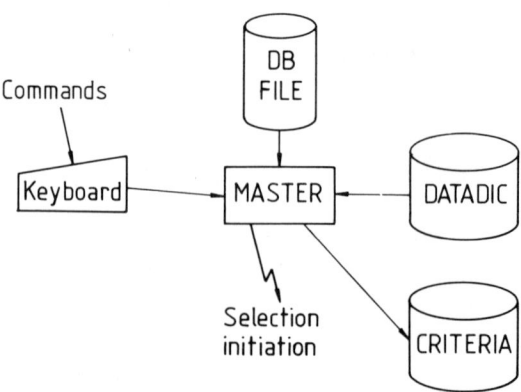

Fig. 4.6

will send the selected fields or totals to the VDU, to a file or to a disk in printing format (lineprinter or teletype).

The field numbers (fields belonging to selected records) required to be output on the VDU, the paper, or to a file (DIS for display).

An option represented by a one or two digit number which is used to indicate to the processing program certain possible choices of methods of execution (OPT for option).

So, for example, it will be possible to give several different meanings to the selection word:

option 00 (taken by default, the most common meaning): If there is a selection criterion on the indexed field 14 (such as SEL 14 (3) = 6), we shall look for the record having the 3rd element of field 14 equal to 6.

option 01: if there is a selection criterion on field 14, ignore the index value, search *all* elements of this field and see if one satisfies the condition.

### 4.1.4.2 *Syntactic and Semantic Peculiarities*

A field may be indexed. Its number is then followed by a left (open) parenthesis, the value (position) to be considered, and a right (closed) parenthesis.

When necessary, the different selection language instructions or a series of field names are separated by spaces.

The language is developed for loading from cards, from a terminal or from a file generated by a program that has decided to perform a selection (under the control of the MASTER program). The various keywords (SEL, DIS, TOT, OPT, OUT) form recognizable syntactic units (verbs). To identify the destination of the output as being on paper when output is initiated from a terminal, the OUT P verb must be followed by a text string in quotation marks making up a title to be printed at the head of the listing. The title tells the operator the name of the person to whom the output belongs, for example.

The output file produced by OUT F has a *universal* format independent of the database. It contains records of eight numeric fields and two alphanumeric fields. The numeric fields are signed and have a 'sufficient' capacity (13 digits for example). The alphanumeric fields have capacities of 25 and six characters respectively. The file is used to receive fields designated by the instruction.

DIS field number, field number, · · ·

For each selected record, we create one record in the output file.

The file is intended for 'automatic statistics' described in the following sections of this chapter.

The format of the display screen and paper output is controlled by automatic paging. Absence of the 'DIS' instruction indicates that it is necessary to display all fields, and is only used for files which have few fields or for the printed listing.

A SEL ALL instruction indicates a selection without criteria. It is used most often to obtain totals or counts calculated by using all the logical records of the database. It is sometimes used to copy one or more fields in the output file for each database record.

### 4.1.4.3 Pictorial Representation of Selection Syntax

The following representation contains two types of symbol:

entities surrounded by

horizontal and vertical arrows    →       ↓

designates a primitive symbol (reserved word) which cannot be subdivided. You can compare it with a letter of the alphabet which is used to define more complex entities.

*Example 4.2*

OPT  designates the group of three letters OPT and introduces the OPT verb (option)

A  designates the letter A

empty  designates the possible absence of the element of which it is a component

designates a composite entity which can be described in terms of elementary symbols, e.g.

OPTION

designates a composite entity. The definition must be searched for elsewhere and will be in the form

→  (horizontal arrow) indicates continuation. The example:

SEL — SPACE — ALL

shows that the elementary symbol SEL must be followed by a SPACE (defined as such) which must be followed by the elementary symbol ALL.

↓ (vertical arrow) indicates the possibility of subdivision, for example,

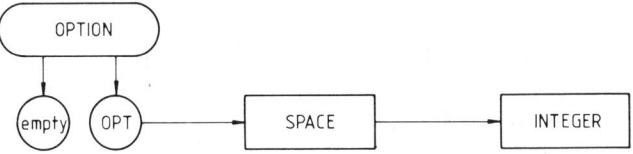

shows that the 'option' entity can be reduced to:

1) empty (no option: 'option' is optional), or
2) the basic symbol OPT followed by a space followed by an integer.

### 4.1.4.4 Recursive Definition

When we represent graphically the fact that a text string is a series of one or more characters we proceed as follows (below and Figs. 4.7, 4.8 and 4.9):

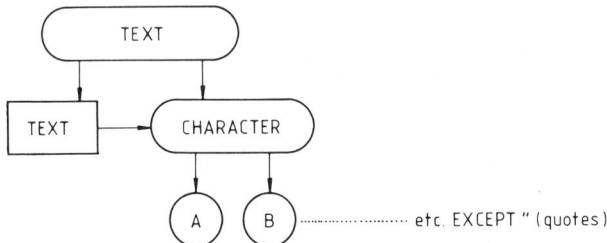

The right-hand vertical arrow says that a text string may be a (single) character. The left-hand vertical arrow says that a text string may be a text string (defined elsewhere, page   ) followed by a character.

Therefore a text string can be a character followed by a character, or two characters, or a text string (of two characters) followed by a third character, etc. This type of definition is said to be recursive. There is no limit on the definition of the entity. In practice we shall limit text strings to 132 for example, and integers to 11 digits.

### 4.1.4.5 Points Concerning Graphical Representation

This representation (also called a syntactic map) defines a set of instructions. Only the syntax is defined, that is to say the set of all possible combinations of characters allowed. The representation defines neither the *semantics* (that is, the meaning) nor the *limitations* such as:

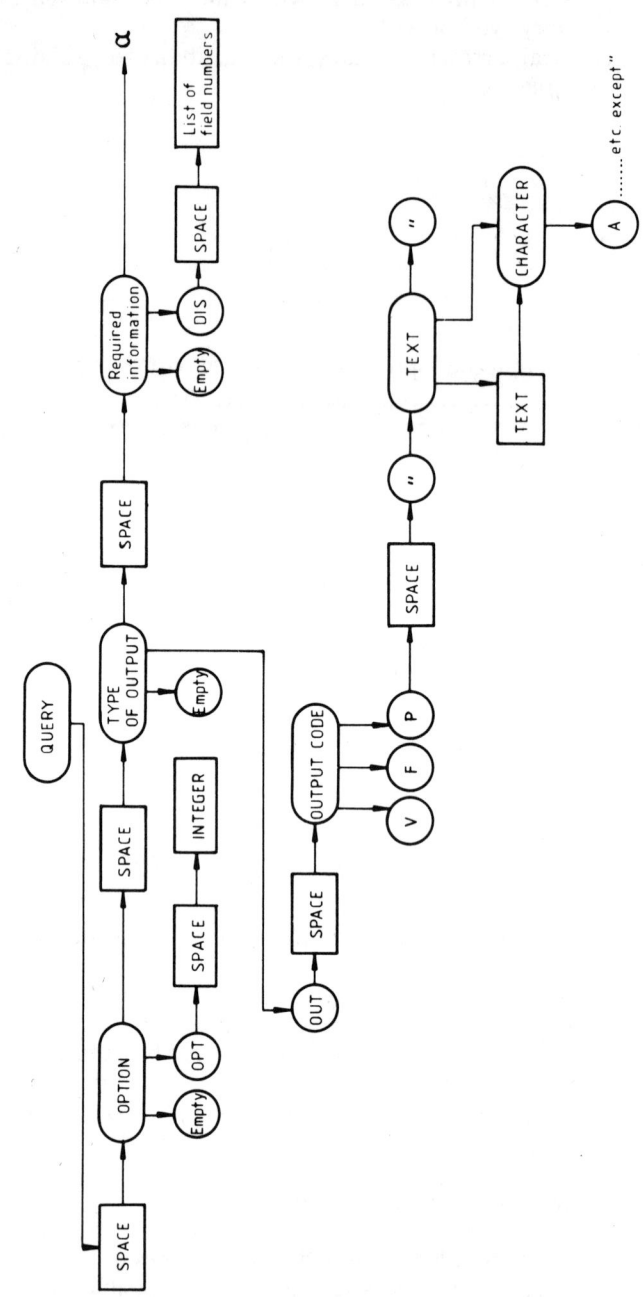

120

Fig. 4.7

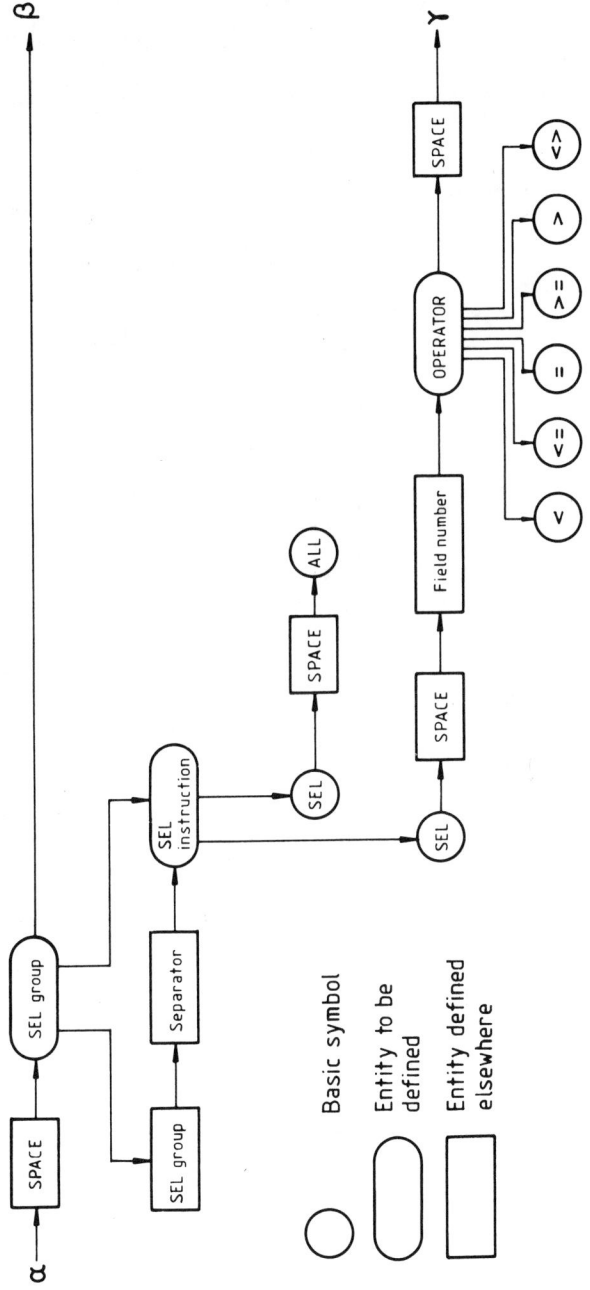

Basic symbol

Entity to be
defined

Entity defined
elsewhere

Fig. 4.8

121

122

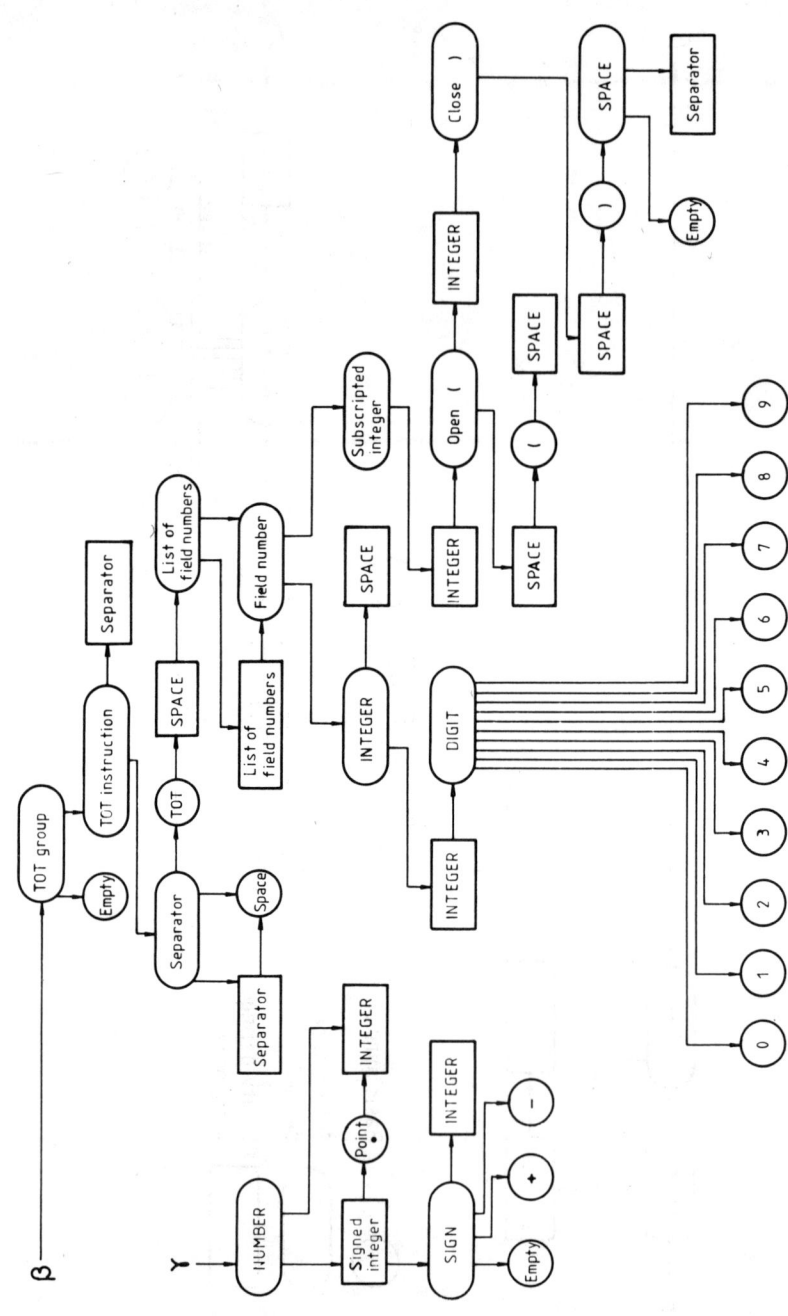

Fig. 4.9

number of SEL instructions in the SEL group;
number of fields in a list of field numbers;
text length, integer length;
maximum value of a subscript (integer enclosed by parentheses), etc.

This representation has two main advantages:

clarity: it is easy to see at a glance which syntactic constructions are allowed;
modularity: a small compiler can be written (capable of recognizing this syntax and translating it into a coded form (which is easy for a program to interpret) by defining subprograms for most of the simple entities. Thus we shall create a subprogram capable of recognizing a SPACE (empty or string of spaces), another to recognize an integer, another (which uses the previous one) to recognize a decimal number, etc.

The compiler for the selection syntax above was written in this way in COBOL in 4 days and perfected in 4 hours. It can be executed in 9000 bytes of memory. Readers who intend to extend the syntax could write the compiler as an automaton. As this method is widely taught today we shall not describe it here.

### 4.1.4.6 Notes on the Fundamental Operations other than Selection

The most complicated processor of the data manipulation language is the one that handles SELection. We give below a few brief indications on how the other operations are described.

#### 4.1.4.6.1 Zero
This operation is used for the initial creation of the database, in principle once only, so we are concerned with a specific set of programs. In certain cases where the data exist already, on magnetic tape for example, this set of programs creates the database from the tape. In other cases the data are created on cards in the same format as subsequent additions; the zero operation then consists of creating the database file(s) and initializing the header fields (creation date, address of the first available record, etc); the + − programs load the database. There is therefore no particular syntax for the zero operation.

#### 4.1.4.6.2 − +
This operation is used for adding entire records (or details within an open item structure). Whatever the storage device (cards, or tape), each record (or detail) to be added must consist of three parts:

the identification field (record number for example);
the operation code ( + or − symbol);
the fields to be added (the whole record or the detail).

When we are concerned with subtraction, this part is used only for intended

123

redundancy, to verify the identification. The cards (tape or · · ·) are read by the specific programs for the − + operation on the database in question.

### 4.1.4.6.3 MOD
In each record, the properties of accessibility and generality mean that we must be able to modify the contents of every field except one; the identifier—that is, the field that identifies the record and is contained in the base index file. This field cannot be modified. To change it, it is necessary to destroy and recreate the record ( − +). All the other fields can be modified by using records of the form:

identification (record number for example) which designates the record to which the field to be modified belongs;
the field to be modified (field number and index (if it exists));
new value (numeric or alphanumeric).

### 4.1.4.6.4 RES
As well as restructuring, sorting, and database reorganization, which we do not need to describe, the function of the restructuring operation in history type structures is to delete records that are no longer valid. These are described by a characteristic field number (date for example) and the reference value, which defines what is 'no longer valid'.

### 4.1.4.6.5 + F
Addition (or subtraction) of data types GF, F, D→, DG→ or P is not strictly an operation of the same type as those previously described. This one deals with the database evolution. It concerns the data description language (abbreviated to DDL). It is possible, however, to initiate an operation of this type by using the data manipulation language (abbreviated to DML). The syntax is then:

'DB name' '+ F'

Updating the data dictionary is sometimes followed by a reorganization (restructuring operation) of the database.

### 4.1.4.6.6 + →
The points above concerning + F also apply to + →; this operation, initiated by the data manipulation language, updates the data dictionary, and is followed by the creation of a new copy of the database.

### 4.1.4.6.7 + I
Addition (or destruction) of a secondary index can be done without making another copy of the database. The syntax is:

'DB name' '+ I' 'field number (index)'
'file name (s) index storage type' 'parameters for these fields'.

124

### 4.1.5 Controlling Access to a Database: The 'Window' Principle

When several programs have to access a database, the following problems arise:
1.  The description of the database file structure and methods of searching (SEL) and updating have the advantage of being unique. We shall use libraries whenever possible; a library is a series of instructions (COBOL for example) describing the structure and the subprogram(s) for access to the database. Libraries are created by a *simple* program and used to compile *all the other* programs. So we obtain uniqueness of file names and descriptions, and modes of access; moreover, when the file description or file access mode is modified, only the single program which creates the libraries need be modified and the others recompiled. We say that the database access via the compiled form of the libraries, is through a unique window, in this case a *source language window*.
2.  When a program is run, some computers allow subprograms that are compiled separately to be loaded with the program. For all programs requiring access to the database, it is advantageous to reserve access to a unique group of such subprograms. This method, called *object language window,* is better than the previous one because:
    user programs do not have to be recompiled when a modification is made to the structure or access mode. Only independently compiled subprograms change, and link-editing must be redone.
    On some computers, programs can be written in assembly language and used in conjunction with programs written in a high level language. Assembly language gives an improved *performance* (execution speed) or improved *accessibility* (bit-access for example). These subprograms can allow the packing/unpacking of data at the same time as the retrieval or updating of data; the database is thus viewed 'directly' by the programs using this window.
3.  When access to the database is made in a multiprogramming environment (with or without time-sharing) a problem of access conflict arises: If a program A reads record E, then program B reads the same record E, and then A modifies E, and B modifies E; the result is as if only B had modified E—modification by A has been 'ignored': there is an *access conflict*. When the computer operating system does not provide suitable access protection, whether it is non-existent, too flexible or too restrictive (preventing for example two reads without simultaneous update) we resort to a *regulating window*.
    This is made up of a single program which holds exclusive access to the database. This program communicates with user programs via 'mailbox'. Each user program has its own mailbox (small file or memory area equally accessible by the window program). The program stores its requests (read/write) in the mailbox, and receives replies from it. The window program keeps a count of the requests, satisfying them while preventing access conflicts. Let us note that requests are not necessarily processed in their order of arrival. The program tries to minimize disk access and groups the requests according to the criteria whenever possible. The regulating window optimizes disk accessing at the same time.

### 4.1.5.1 Creation of a Regulating/Optimizing Window

The method introduced above produces a window program, and is suitable for systems where several dozen logical access channels to a database may be required. This is the case for example in real-time order-processing systems with many terminals; each sale must produce an item stock update and must prevent simultaneous sales of the same item.

Another method suitable for systems where access conflicts are rare, considering the number of terminals that are likely to access a database at any one time, is the *monitor* program. This program does not act like the window program at the record (or block) level of a database; it controls access to the entire database. For the monitor, each program is characterized by the files or database that it accesses and for each file or database by two parameters:

the *access* to the file (read or read/write or append);
the *type of access allowed* to other programs (none, read only, or read and write or append).

The monitor allows or inhibits the running of each program submitted, according to the possible conflicts defined by the access allowed to files being used by programs already running. Note that with the access above we can associate the idea of 'appending', which consists of adding *new* records at the end of an existing file without affecting existing records. The idea of conflict is thus transferred from existing records to the end of file *position*, which varies when there are several simultaneous additions.

Note also that the window concept (object window, window program, monitor program) can equally be used to control access to a database with respect to the 'secrecy', checking to see if the requesting program has the required 'permission'.

The window concept 'through which an application program sees a database' can also be applied as a neat method of solving the problem of *flexibility*, that is to say the ability of the database to evolve with respect to the number, type and nature of its information. This concerns the *mask window*. A mask window is a program P which has exclusive access to the database. P receives transactions from application programs A, B, and C (through memory or via a file). Each transaction passes a code from A, B, or C to P, designating: the fundamental operation to be performed ($-$ $+$, MOD, SEL), a whole record for '$+$', or field numbers for MOD and SEL (to be modified or supplied), if necessary the selection criteria to obey. The transfer format is *standard*, independent of the record format of the database.

The program P then processes the transaction (including packing/unpacking, regulation, optimization, privacy) and replies to the requesting program A, B, or C. The reply is also made in a *standard* format.

In short, each application program passes to P only the fields it knows and receives the fields it needs. This is done using a standard format.

As a result, the evolution of a database requires only the modification (recompilation) of P. *This is a very important point.* Given a mask window, even a closed database can evolve easily.

126

There are two ways of creating a mask window:
1. The DBMS (database management system) which is one program (integrated into the operating system) used for all databases on the system.
2. As many mask-windows as databases. This approach is often the most efficient and most simple to create from the point of view of analysis / programming. It is particularly well suited to minicomputers, where available resources (memory size, power of the operating system, disk space, etc.) prevent the use of a general database management system.

### 4.1.6 Integrating Several Databases

#### 4.1.6.1 Definition

Let us consider a number of databases that we shall call components.

Integration of these databases consists of carrying out a logical connection, thus obtaining one database, which is said to be integrated. We are not concerned with performing a physical connection (for example by using common files).

*Note*: In general, the difficulty in designing a data processing program increases much more quickly than the number of data fields we want it to handle.

For example, it is easier to design ten small programs with one parameter than one program with ten parameters, when the parameters are not independent. After solving the ten design problems of the small programs, it is easy to solve an eleventh problem: integrating them. The best illustration of this is well known; it is much easier to develop modular software than non-modular software. With databases it is easier to develop and use small databases, even if there are several of them, than one big database.

Thus, for example, rather than developing a massive commercial database consisting of 500 or so pieces of information, it is wiser to develop five separate databases—customers, items, orders, invoice history, payments. These can be developed one after the other, each having its own nucleus. Next we must take care to integrate them using the methods below. This will prove easier than constructing an integrated database directly. From an organization standpoint, it makes very little sense to try to specify, then design and implement, one huge company-wide database instead of five or ten small databases in succession.

The first step of such a vast project would be to write a functional specifications document. In such a document, most of the company's administrative activities would be described, in their data processing dimension. Many people would have to be interviewed, many organization charts drawn to represent the flows of information through the administrative circuits.

The project leader would have to identify and document in a data dictionary hundreds of pieces of information. This first step would take many months. And by the time the specifications are written, approved and budgeted, it is possible that something will have changed in the organization, or that top management will have become tired of waiting for the project to get off the ground. The next steps will produce complex software, with time-consuming imple-

127

mentation and debugging problems. And last but not least, the project would bring about a considerable change in the habits, in *most* administrative habits of *many* people—a considerable amount of dissatisfaction, frustration and opposition may result, especially if the software is not perfect from the start.

It is, therefore, necessary to implement small, quick-to-install, easy-to-master databases: for instance, these may reside in distinct connectable or microcomputers. In addition, it often happens that we wish to integrate databases constructed separately.

### 4.1.6.2 Redundancy Problem

Integrated databases have inevitably a logical connection; in general, one or more pieces of information will belong to several databases. It is sometimes worthwhile to use physical connections (pointers) to integrate the separate databases.

Databases linked by pointers obviously allow rapid navigation from one to another. But the physical pointers have a major inconvenience: they are time-consuming to update and restructure. Therefore, we have to allow for the *regeneration* of the pointers, a useful step should pointers be destroyed due to a system crash, software or operating fault, or power failure.

### 4.1.6.3 Fundamental Operations on Integrated Databases

Each database component has its own nucleus. Thus for each we have modules adapted for creation and maintenance. There is no point in abandoning the nucleus components, but we should create a *master nucleus* which uses them to give the properties of an integrated database. The aim of the master nucleus is to filter data going to (and coming from) the modules of the nucleus components. The filtering consists of formating and logical verification. Seen through the master nucleus, disjoint databases appear to be integrated.

Important note: Combining databases increases the number of fields. It will usually be necessary to design the modules of the master nucleus in the form of a 'window'. Thus, only the necessary information will be sent to and received from outside the nucleus. Moreover, the format used will be standard. The master nucleus forming a window can easily be used with fixed format modules performing the fundamental operations of component databases.

### 4.1.6.4 Search Path and Transfers

Selection on an integrated database poses the problem of knowing in which order to search through component bases. This is because of redundancy. For example, let us suppose that the 'customer number' field belongs to the first base (customer master file) and to the second (invoice history file).

Moreover, let us suppose that we want to find the customer name and address of 'wholesale' customers who have invoices of over $5000 in the invoice history file. Then suppose that the name and address are only in the customer file, that the 'wholesaler/retailer' code appears in both component bases, and that the invoiced amount appears only in the invoice history file. How does the machine know:

if it should scan through the customer file, then, for each wholesale customer, search for his invoices; or

if it should scan through the invoice history file and, for each wholesale invoice of over $5000 search for the name and address of the customer?

This example illustrates the necessity of providing the master nucleus with the questions to put to each of the selection module components:

1. The order in which searching should be carried out (base I then base II, etc.). We call this the search path, navigation or traverse.
2. the *transfers* of information to be carried out between the search modules. For example, after finding the name and address of a wholesale customer in the customer base, transfer the customer number to the invoice history selection module and use it as a search key. Note that these transfers can involve logical information (key such as customer number) or physical information (pointer linking two bases).

### 4.1.6.5 Conclusion

The list of requirements developed above is a basis for the construction of a master module.

Whatever the fundamental operation that this master module carries out, it will use the specialized modules of the component bases as 'submodules' or 'slaves'. Integration of bases is thus made possible by the master nucleus (set of master modules) and not by the physical integration of data. It often happens that, when we already have the slave nuclei and we create a master nucleus, the creation is easy to analyse and perfect. The only serious problem which arises, as for any nucleus, is that of simultaneous processing of several transactions, coming from several programs executing concurrently. A solution to this problem exists and is known as *multi threading*.

The solution can be found by using:

1. input/output queues of messages from the master nucleus and component nuclei. This solution has the disadvantage that it only processes one message at a time;
2. several copies of each module and the multiprogramming capability of the computer. This second solution which is much more efficient, but requires, however, that the computer initiate the modules automatically when more than one transaction must be processed at a time. This initiation is performed by a specialized monitor program, after a non-conflict verification.

Note: The most powerful among commercial database management systems use I/O queues and re-entrance; for instance IBM's 'IMS'.

## 4.2 SOME PROGRAMMING TECHNIQUES

### 4.2.1 Binary Search

Binary search is a method which can be applied to arrays (in memory) or files (disk). Data are arranged in increasing order and no data item exists more than once. The method takes advantage of the order of the array to avoid searching right through it (that is, all elements one after the other); it solves the following problem: 'in a table T of N elements, find the element which is equal to a given element X'.

We shall designate the elements of rank $1, 2, \cdots, I, \cdots, N$ in T by T(1) T(2) $\cdots$ T(I) $\cdots$ T(N). The method consists of finding the rank R of element T(R) = X (if it exists) by surrounding it with (variable) elements T(A) and T(B) which will become *closer and closer* to X. The convergence of A and B is achieved by successively dividing the segment AB into 2:

1. We start with A = 1 and B = N (N: size of the array)
   if X < T(A) or X > T(N), X is not in T: exit
2. Calculate M = (A + B)/2: M is the middle position in T. Integer division is used (M is exactly in the middle if A + B is even).
   If X = T(M), R = M, exit
   if X < T(M) R is between A and M. $A \leqslant R < M$
   if X > T(M) R is between M and B. $M < R \leqslant B$

So we have decreased the interval to half the interval: AM or MB; B becomes equal to M or A becomes equal to M and we go back to stage 2. The process is repeated as long as the size of the interval AB is greater than 1.

Then X = T(A) and R = A or
   X = T(B) and R = B or
   X is not in T: end.

This method of search is extremely useful, especially in searching index tables.

### 4.2.2 Improved Binary Search

The binary search method described above requires a divide-by-2 operation (or multiply by 0.5) for each iteration. Some computers execute these operations very slowly. A typical minicomputer that can carry out a comparison in 6 microsecond ($\mu$s) takes 40 microseconds ($\mu$s) to add two numbers and almost 1000 microseconds ($\mu$s) to multiply or divide! On such machines searching by binary search is often slower than simply searching through the whole table.

The improved binary search method, which avoids additions and divisions, can then be used advantageously; its inconvenience is that memory requirements are greater because of the number of instructions it requires. The principle relies on a simple observation: if the array T has a very small number of elements (for example N = 8) the search can be completely programmed because the results of the operations of the type M = (A + B)/2 are known *a priori*.

1. If $X < T(1)$ or $X > T(8)$ X is not in T, exit.
2. If $X = T(5)$: R = 5, exit.
   If $X < T(5)$:
       If $X = T(3)$ R = 3, exit.
       If $X < T(3)$:
         If $X = T(2)$ R = 2, exit.
         If $X < T(2)$
           If $X = T(1)$ R = 1, exit.
           Otherwise X is not in T
         If $X > T(2)$ X is not in T.
       If $X > T(3)$
         If $X = T(4)$ R = 4, exit
         Otherwise X is not in T.
   If $X > T(5)$
       If $X = T(7)$ R = 7, exit.
       If $X < T(7)$:
         If $X = T(6)$ R = 6, exit.
         Otherwise X is not in T.
       If $X > T(7)$:
         If $X = T(8)$ R = 8, exit.
         Otherwise X is not in T.

Suppose that T has $8 \times 8 = 64$ elements; the search can take place in two stages.

*First stage*: Build an array R2 of eight elements taking the elements of rank 1, 9, 17, 25, 33, 41, 49, 57 on which an improved binary search as described above is performed. If X is found, exit. If not, find in which interval (2 to 8, 10 to 16, · · ·, 58 to 64) X would be. Perform stage 2.

*Second stage*: Build an array T3 of eight elements with the elements of the interval found. We then perform a new improved binary search and then have the final result. Of course, building the array T3 is not done with eight programmed transfers but with one single transfer of adequate length and address. This requires one multiplication (one per stage from the second).

We see that with three stages the method allows us to search an array of $8^3 = 512$ elements. It is also clear that we do not have to build arrays of eight elements. Other dimensions are all right but it is advisable to make the dimensions powers of 2. When the array T has an arbitrary size (491, for example) the methods requires that the higher number elements be completed for arrays T2, T3, etc. that are created by *inaccessible* values (High-Value in Cobol for example).

### 4.2.3 How to Design a Data Selection Program

We give here some general advice on how to create a data selection program for a closed database; the reader can extend these principles described for open databases by using the modular techniques described in section 3.6.3.5 in Chapter 3.

### 4.2.3.1 General Architecture

Data selection uses the most rapid access method available. We first look for the selection criteria fields that have an access index file to accelerate access. If several such fields are found, the one with the highest level index is kept; this search is the fastest because of the condensed structure of the index. In the absence of a field appearing in an index, we must search the file sequentially; if an existence table (one or a few bits per record) exists we can use it, otherwise it is necessary to search through the data. Then, if an index is used, we can determine the search interval with the help of the selection criteria related to the field described.

*Example 4.3* Consider an invoice history database and a selection which searches for the total turnover of item number 261400 for March. Suppose that the database has an index-by-invoice date (in other words, the invoices are stored in order of date). Of the required criteria (item = 261400, date $\geqslant$ 1 March, date $<$ 1 April) two refer to the date which appears in the index. We search the index for the positions of the first and last invoices for March in the database file (we call these positions MINI and MAXI). The search interval will be MINI to MAXI and we read it sequentially. The first part of the data selection program is designed to find the search interval while verifying the given criteria and opening the input–output files. When we have virtual memory management this is the first program segment (overlay).

When the database is not sorted on the criteria appearing in the index, the MINI–MAXI idea has no meaning for the database itself but still has a meaning for the index, which is read sequentially in the MINI–MAXI interval. For each record satisfying the criteria-index, we check that it satisfies the other criteria as well. This technique is particularly useful when existence tables are available. The second segment of the program contains the search loop, with three modules:

- an input module used to feed the other two modules with candidate records (satisfying the index-criteria if there is one);
- a comparison module which verifies that the set of given selection criteria is (or is not) satisfied by the given record;
- an output module that makes a copy of the required fields of output to the designated file (or display screen or printer) in the required format. This module also calculates any totals which may be required.

The third and last segment is reserved for the closing of files and operations prior to the end of the program. A selection program does not contain, in general, code which is capable of syntactic analysis of the selection part of the data manipulation language. This analysis, which is required whatever the database, is performed by a specialized program that translates the selection instructions into code transmitted to the specific selection program of the database. When possible, transmission is done with the help of a memory area common to both programs; by default a small file will be used.

## 4.2.3.2 Design of Comparison and Output Modules: Use of the 'Computed GO TO'

In high level languages (FORTRAN, COBOL, BASIC, etc.) we have an instruction known as the computed GO TO, which is useful for carrying out in a simple way the choice of the required fields.

### 4.2.3.2.1 Comparison Module

The idea of this module is to check if the present record satisfies all the required criteria. We shall suppose that we have received from the syntax analyser the following codes:

Field number (1 to . . .);
Subscript (1 to . . ., 0 if the field is not subscripted);
Relation: 1 for $<$
         2 for $\leqslant$
         3 for $=$
         4 for $\geqslant$
         5 for $>$
         6 for $\neq$
Reference value (number with sign)

These relations are examined by the subprogram TEST-FIELD which receives the contents of the field to be tested (subscripted or not) via the variable CANDIDATE, the code (1 to 6) from the relation in the variable OPERATOR and the corresponding reference value in REFERENCE (see Fig. 4.10).

To supply the *candidate* variables with field contents, we use the computed GO TO. If for example the database contains 40 fields of which field 26 is subscripted, and fields 1, 2, 4, 9, 17, 25, 38 and 40 may not be selected (alphanumeric) we use a COBOL construction like:

```
GO TO

E    E    S3   E    S5   S6   S7   S8   E    S10
S11  S12  S13  S14  S15  S16  E    S18  S19  S20
S21  S22  S23  S24  E    S26  S27  S28  S29  S30
S31  S32  S33  S34  S35  S36  S37  E    S39  E
DEPENDING ON FIELD-NUMBER.
E.   GO  TO  FIELD-NUMBER-FALSE.
S3.    MOVE NITEM TO CANDIDATE GO TO NEXT.
S5.    MOVE PRICE TO CANDIDATE GO TO NEXT.
..................................................
S.26.  MOVE ACCOUNT (I) TO CANDIDATE GO TO
NEXT.
```

············································································

NEXT.   MOVE OPER TO OPERATOR.
        MOVE VALREF TO REFERENCE.
        PERFORM TEST-FIELD.
In the above example:

E, S3, S5 . . . S39 are labels (also called paragraph names or addresses).
FIELD-NUMBER-FALSE is the label for processing relations referring to disallowed fields.

NITEM, PRICE, ACCOUNT, are variables describing the database record fields in question.

I is the subscript given for the ACCOUNT field.

PERFORM is the calling instruction for the subprogram TEST-FIELD.

The comparison module is therefore a loop WILL call TEST-FIELD as many times as there are relations to check, supplying it with values as above. On exit from the loop, the reply is either 'accepted' or 'rejected'.

### 4.2.3.2.2 Output module
The module receives an indication of the field numbers (possibly indexed) to transfer to the output. These transfers are carried out by the normal assignment

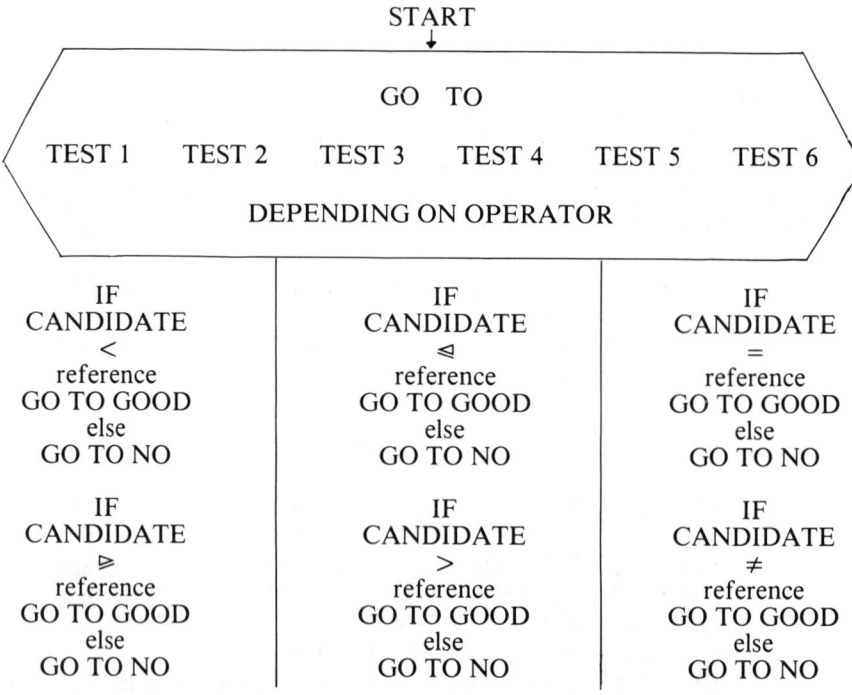

Fig. 4.10   'COBOL-style' flow-diagram of TEST-FIELD.

134

instruction (= in FORTRAN, MOVE in COBOL) within a loop which is executed once for each field to be transferred.

The choice of the instruction to be used also depends on a computed GO TO which transfers control to the transfer instruction for the equivalent variable. Do not forget to allow for the output corresponding to SEL ALL.

### 4.2.3.3 Notes on Selection Programs

All such programs are similar. Writing the first one takes a long time, the second one less time, and the third becomes easier, and so on.

Selection can have several meanings (see 'OPTION' section 4.1.4.3) For each meaning there will be a single corresponding comparison module. Some fields corresponding to calculated results are not stored in the database but may appear as the selectable fields; this is the case with fields corresponding to values (price multiplied by quantity) or some totals.

The use of assembly language makes it possible to avoid the use of the computed GO TO. We can then use a table which associates with each field its begin address and length in the record, and transfer any field with the same instruction.

It is easy to add two more set-oriented relations to the six above ($<$, $\leqslant$, $=$, $\geqslant$, $>$, $\neq$): $\in$ (belongs to) and $\notin$ (does not belong to) numbered 7 and 8 respectively. A special binary search routine then checks to see if CANDIDATE belongs or does not belong to the set (indicated by the reference value).

### 4.2.4 Automatic Reporting and Statistics

There is one type of selection that cannot be performed in a single pass. This is a selection which involves a total, an average or a number of records. For example we wish to find the customer who has made the greatest number of orders (and this number is not stored and kept up to date); or we wish to find the average invoice total for a customer belonging to a given customer category; or we wish to find a distribution of customers by turnover for a certain item. We must first of all carry out a summation by customer, then a selection according to the required criteria, and then possibly a graphical representation on a screen or printer; histogram, curve, cumulative frequency curve, etc.

The following method, which is easy to implement and is independent of the database, allows these types of statistics to be obtained automatically. Each selection program, whichever database it searches, includes a *standard* format output field. This file (selection file) SELF has identical records irrespective of the database, which is grouped in identical blocks. Each record contains for example:

  seven signed numeric fields of eleven figures before the decimal point and four after;
  one 'large' alphanumeric field of 25 characters;
  one 'small' alphanumeric field of nine characters.

For each selected record, there is a corresponding SELF record to which the desired fields are transferred. A standard sort program sorts SELF (producing a file SELF2 with the same structure) on a key corresponding to the first numeric field (or perhaps the first two numeric fields). A standard summation program reads the sorted file SELF2 and performs a summation using field 1 for level-breaks (or field 1 with field 2 giving subtotals), of fields 2, 3, 4, 5, 6, 7 or just some of these fields. The totals and subtotals produce a file SELF3 of identical structure to that of SELF and SELF2. In file SELF4 a standard selection program creates a subset of SELF3 obeying certain criteria; for example, there will be a selection on a *total*. Then, a standard statistics program will produce the curve, histogram, average etc., in other words, the required statistics (see Fig. 4.11).

### 4.2.4.1 Statistics Program Architecture

The statistics program performs the calculations in two passes; reading SELF4 twice. Its organization is as follows:

1. First pass: reading SELF4 in order to determine for each field, the minimum, maximum, total and the number of records in SELF4.
2. Calculating the average values of the fields; the division into intervals of that field used for variable $X$ according to the given parameters.
3. Second pass: reading SELF4 and assigning each value of the variable(s) $Y$ to an interval $X$; counting the number of $Y$'s for each $X$; calculating the average differences of the field values (enabling us to calculate the standard deviation and the variance).
4. Determining the $Y$ scales (one scale per $Y$ function to be represented).
5. Output to paper or screen as required.

Note: Alphanumeric fields in SELF files (not previously mentioned) are used for a special type of statistic which is very frequently used for printing totals (even subtotals) and corresponding headings.

*Example 4.4* The specialized selection transfers into SELF

in field 1, the customer number;
in field 2, the amount of each invoice;
in field 8, (alphanumeric), the customer name.

We can print the invoice total for each customer with his name and number.

### 4.2.4.2 Using Standard (SELF) Files for Relational Processing

A SELF file can be considered as being a *set* of records, provided that no two records are identical with respect to a *key* (defined as an ordered group of fields).

We shall not cover here the definitions of all relational operations, defined in 'relational algebra'. However, we can define three *simple* operations to demonstrate the possibilities brought about by the SELF file approach. In all three operations, both the input and output files have the same SELF format; an output file can subsequently be used as input to another operation.

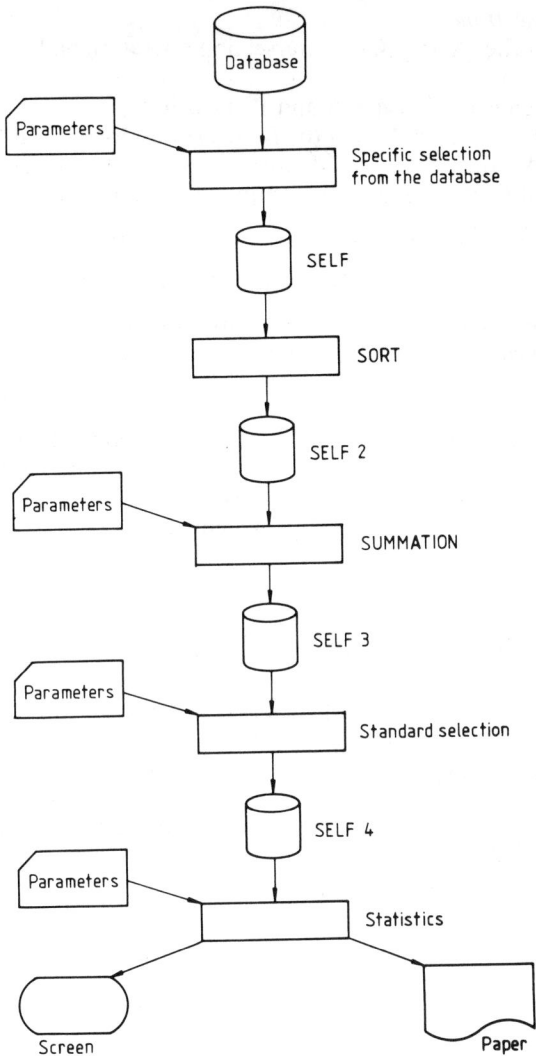

Fig. 4.11

#### 4.2.4.2.1 Projection

Given an input file with $N$ fields, projection builds an output file with one output record for each input record. The output record has $M < N$ fields. This operation is used to do away with fields which are no longer necessary after some operations (often alphanumeric fields). Note that projection can produce an output file which is *not* a set, as records may have become identical after removing $N-M$ fields.

*4.2.4.2.2 Intersection*

Given two input files A and B, the intersection operation builds an output file C such that:

- a record which exists in *both* A and B exists in C;
- a record which exists in A only (or B only) does not exist in C;
- records in A, B and C are identified by their (unique) keys–however, a record of C may have fields coming from A and B.

The set (C) is the intersection of sets (A) and (B):

$$(C) = (A) \cap (B)$$

It is very easy to write an intersection program, provided that A and B have previously been sorted on their common key.

*Example 4.5*

- A contains the total quantity on order of items coming from an 'items on order' database. Each record of A is uniquely associated to an item;
- B contains the items with a zero (out-of-stock) inventory.
- C = A ∩ B will contain the items which cannot be shipped and must be replenished.

## 4.3 DATABASE DEVELOPMENT PROCEDURE

This section contains list of helpful suggestions concerning the definition (specification), organic analysis, programming and implementation of a database. The list is organized like a procedure and discusses the actions to be undertaken in the order that they must be carried out. This is not, however, an exhaustive list—far from it; the essential points concerning databases in particular are covered, rather than other computer applications.

### 4.3.1 Specifications

It is clear that the first step in starting the design and implementation of a database is the specification. In general, the database concerns more people than would any ordinary application. We need to know, answer and note carefully the following questions:

1. What are the aims of the design and use of the database?
2. Who are the intended users (persons, departments)? What is their position? How does information circulate among them (documents, procedures, volumes, sequence).
3. What is the expected life of the database? In general a lifetime of less than 3 years does not justify high costs of writing programs, gathering a lot of data, training personnel, installing hardware.
4. What sort of data will be used? We are not concerned here with the precise definition (which is done after specification approval) but with defining the scope of the subject.

5. What are, in general terms, the usage plan and the personnel (responsible departments):

for the initial data creation,
for subsequent updating,
for each expected type of use.

(by plan we mean a logical scheme describing the information paths and linking the users, processes and data).

6. How often is the database used? In particular how often is a quick response required (interrogation via a terminal) real-time processing (etc.)?
7. How much privacy of information is required? Does this depend on the type of data and the people who have access?
8. What level of safety (data integrity guarantee) is required? How can we recover from a system crash, a loss of data? How can data integrity be verified?
9. How valuable is the service to the firm (if it is possible to evaluate it financially or otherwise)? What is the maximum budget foreseen

to create the database?
to operate the database?

### 4.3.2 Defining the Data to be Used: Data Dictionary

Once the specifications have been approved, a list of pieces of data and associated definitions can be drawn up. This list is obtained by working backwards from the expected results in the specification, to arrive at the data required to obtain them. We can determine two classes of data: those data items which must be stored, and those which must be reconstructed by calculation. The non-redundancy principle will ideally reduce the quantity of the first class in favour of the second; for a first approximation we shall not allow any redundancy, so a minimum of redundant data is stored. This is necessary for good performance and safety in case of loss of pointers.

The expected results may be individual pieces of information, like a quantity in stock, or group of related data like a parts list. The method described in Chapter 3, section 3.6.3 is used to break down the groups (reports, CRT displays, etc.)—identifying subgroups, individual data items, their interrelationships and levels.

Among the data to be stored, it is a good idea to try and distinguish those items that are the most 'important' (that is, those most frequently used or with the shortest response times) from those which may be stored on magnetic tape and only occasionally used, and from those which by their stability, size of distribution should be on microfiche or paper. Here we are concerned with the principal storage medium rather than the transmission medium; we cannot often mix one with the other. To prepare the data dictionary without redundancy or omission, it is a good idea to refer to the operational plan described in the specifications that we can write in detail. We can deduce from it the output and the necessary types of information, and then detail the types right down to the elementary data items. The data can be broken down by storage medium.

The results of the data definition is written into a list which gradually becomes the data dictionary. At this level, it is advisable to prepare a list of output reports for the interrogations, and to get it approved by future users at the same time as the precise list of data that they will have to supply; after approval these lists will be appended to the specifications.

### 4.3.3 Defining the Necessary Hardware

When the data to be manipulated, stored and transmitted are well known, it is necessary to express the technical requirements of the database in precise terms: amounts to be stored (disk, tape), the number of transactions to process per day/per month, response time, geographical distribution of users (terminal, if possible), amount printed, amount keyed in (by type: cards, encoder, terminal, etc.) security, recovery, etc. We deduce from the requirements the following computing facilities:

disk space;
number of terminals (by category: display screen, teleprinter);
number of disk channels, processor load, printing capacity.

We must be particularly careful in the determination of the number of disk channels, when there are response-time constraints. An approximate method for arriving at a decision consists of considering the number of transactions per second during peak periods, to count the corresponding average number of disk accesses and transfer volumes, and to carry out tests on the considered computer, so that we can measure the disk transfer rate. Do no forget (if the computer works in time-sharing mode) to count the number of system disk accesses such as virtual memory loading and unloading, 'SWAPPING' of interrupted programs, etc. An average computer system is capable of performing between ten and 100 disk accesses per second depending on the number of independent channels, access speed and number of programs in memory.

A minicomputer using diskettes often has a capacity of two accesses per second. It is advisable to allow a safety margin, if it is necessary to have a good response time and a reasonable reliability in case of a channel or disk failure.

The various results above have to be taken with a certain margin of variation, given the degree of evolution of the database in time. We find that database usage increases more than anticipated, since supply creates demand. (The more answers that are provided, the more questions that are generated.) Conclusions drawn from this investigation should be documented and quantified; very often the resulting budget leads to a revision of the initial objectives! In each case, an approval of the budget is necessary before continuing the study.

### 4.3.4 General System Design

In addition to the 'hardware' budget, we should add those of 'software development and maintenance' and 'operations'. Determination of the 'operations'

140

part is standard; that of the 'software' part relies on a general analysis for which we can indicate characteristics typical of databases.

### 4.3.4.1 Defining Logical Data Groups

Here we are concerned with dividing the set of data into logical groups. The grouping criterion is the *simultaneous use* of certain data items which have the same key in the established operational plans. Thus we can reduce the number of information items manipulated in the rest of the analysis by considering only *groups* of fields; when we are manipulating several hundreds of different fields, this simplification is very valuable. So we can prepare a reduced list of information where each group of fields is followed by its size, frequency of occurrence and its subdivision into elementary fields.

### 4.3.4.2 Defining Physical Files

Knowing what logical groups exist, we can define physical files. The grouping criterion is the usage performance, in the sense of number of disk accesses, disk storage size, search time. It is a pity that a number of analysts continue to use grouping criteria based only on one-to-one relationships. For example, it is not because the postal code and street name are both part of the address (and so have a one-to-one relationship) that it is necessary to group them in the same physical record; the former (small and numeric) may be used for selection criteria, whereas the latter (large and alphanumeric) cannot; and by its presence, the street name increases the size of the record without increasing its usefulness for selections. The grouping criterion is therefore based on processing and storage efficiency, not on logical similarity alone. For processing efficiency it is necessary to consider the set of processes planned in the operational plan, with their frequency and response time. In general terms, there are two approaches to grouping, based on the openness or non-openness of the database. When a decision on this point has to be taken (whether or not leading to the creation of a holdall file), we group together the data as described in the preceding chapter, taking into account their natural hierarchy (for example customer → invoice → payment operations) and the type of database: master file, history or open item.

The *basic* file organization considers the most common mode of access (or the access mode requiring the shortest response time). From this, we deduce the base key and the addressing mode (hash coding, for example). Then we decide whether to have any secondary existence or index tables. Thus, the access hierarchy is *not* designed after the 'natural' hierarchy of the data.

### 4.3.4.3 Appropriate Data Representation and Packing

After constructing the physical files, we must consider whether or not to use data packing. The method of packing will be chosen depending on the machine (bit access, speed of multiplication/division). As far as the bases to be chosen are concerned, we must establish with care the concept of vocabulary/alphabet for each field. The logical groups of fields are generally coded together (multiple-word coding). After taking the various decisions concerning data packing we can make file descriptions final: record sizes, blocking factors, etc.

### 4.3.4.4 Defining the Nucleus

When the files have been defined, we continue with the precise definition of the programs and subprograms comprising the entire nucleus (defined in section 4.1.2). This definition is made by taking into account the operational plan and the window principle. After defining the nucleus, we define the data description and manipulation techniques, as well as the main characteristics of the associated languages or procedures.

### 4.3.4.5 Definiting Application Programs and Interface Data Formats (Window)

After defining the database and the utility software modules, we should define the application programs that produce the required results. This definition, limited to the existence and nature (sort, selection, output, verification, CRT conversation, data entry) can be done fairly quickly.

### 4.3.4.6 Programming Languages

When we can choose between several programming languages it is worth considering the following points:

If we choose to use data packing, we use a language which allows us to write programs most efficiently (assembler, some versions of FORTRAN, PASCAL).
The same applies if we use existence tables (bit manipulation).
It is less expensive to program in a high level language than in assembler; but does this exclude the use of assembler subprograms for operations in which efficiency is of prime importance?
Can we use modules which can be stored in a library, and data transmission between programs via memory?
The number of programmers influences the choice of the application language; today most programmers know COBOL. However, on mini-computers, BASIC is the most serious contender.
Must the database be transferable to another computer with little cost?

Knowing how much software is to be developed, we can estimate the budget, time and personnel necessary, and then obtain approval of these figures.

## 4.3.5 Developing the Nucleus

The first detailed analysis and programming obviously concerns the nucleus. The modules corresponding

to the packing/unpacking operations,
to the fundamental operations (zero, − +, SEL, MOD, RES, +F, + →, + I),
to the data manipulation system, and
to the data description and dictionary system

must be defined in detail at this time, as well as the data input formats and algorithms, data entry, control, restructuring, etc. When the detailed analysis of the nucleus is finished, the database *initial creation* operation must be run. The initial creation process expects data in a certain format according to the creation method chosen (input by cards, or magnetic tapes derived from previous files). Experience shows that data collection, data entry and control represent a lot of work and require considerable time and personnel. This work must start as soon as possible, and continue while the nucleus software is developed. It is a good idea to entrust the overall responsibility for the data supply and control to the person who will eventually be the database administrator, rather than to the person responsible for the programming; the later will only be required to supply the data entry formats, then the software and the initial creation procedures. The arrival of the first data items may or may not coincide with the testing of the nucleus. In any case the nucleus must be thoroughly tested, perfected and made reliable before the application programs can be developed and tested. Thus the selection, modification and subtraction/addition modules will be very useful to the process of testing and debugging the application programs, and then for the correction of possible data entry or software errors. If the database is an open one, changes may occur at least once before the database is put into service for the first time, to allow for any forgotten details.

We must take account of the qualifications of the personnel, who provide the data and use the database in the tests; database concerns more people than a 'classical' application, and the number of possible errors (data and manipulation) is increased. We frequently find that a novice user makes more errors in 1 hour than the most knowledgeable analyst would make in 1 month. If we have not taken the precaution of trying out the database before starting up, even by a procedure simulation without the computer, we are very likely to run into implementation problems. As far as a database is concerned, we should be fully aware of how much more destructive is the innocent imagination of a novice, compared to the imagination of the person concerned with the verification of the validity and integrity of the data.

### 4.3.6 Initial Database Creation

As soon as the nucleus and the initial data are available, we can start to load the database. This operation allows us to test in depth the reliability and the execution time of the fundamental operations. It is quite common for the nucleus to end up modified in one way or another. It is therefore advantageous for the application programs (using the nucleus through the 'window') not to be too complicated for the initial loading, and to use communication areas independent of the database file formats and contents.

### 4.3.7 Application Program Development

Writing application programs calls for only one comment: it is most important to respect the 'window' concept; this is the best way of reducing the costs of program writing, debugging and maintenance, and of making the programs reliable and unaffected by subsequent database evolution.

### 4.3.8 Documentation

Database documentation is one important factor in its correct use, and it is important to see that care is taken in documenting the database management software, because programmers and analysts very often tend to neglect this. We must distinguish between:

- the nucleus documentation (programming, analysis, use of the fundamental operations, safety and security procedures, restart after an error or evolution, data manipulation and definition languages);
- data entry documentation (data entry programs, data entry formats, data entry procedures, list of the validity tests carried out);
- application program documentation (programs, generated printouts and the definition of results printed or obtained by interrogation, validation operation procedures, restart procedures after a crash);
- database administrator documentation (data dictionary and keeping it up to date);
- operations manager documentation (configuration and system software required, frequency of usage operations, applications, maintenance, restructuring, personnel required, budget, execution times, safety procedures);
- documentation for the person responsible for software (map representing all programs written and the associated files nucleus and applications, intended maintenance, budget);
- documentation for users and end-users (interrogation language and procedures).

This documentation cannot be written well if care is not taken *in noting the important points* at the time the decisions are made.